AF413396

EMOTIONAL SELF CARE FOR BLACK WOMEN

Practical techniques to eliminate negative thoughts, healing from trauma and raising self-esteem to achieve happiness and success

Malaika Ndiaye

Copyright 2023 All rights reserved©.

It is strictly forbidden to reproduce, duplicate or transmit the contents of this book without the express written authorization of the author. In no event shall the publisher be held legally responsible for any compensation, damage or monetary loss caused by the information contained in this book, either directly or indirectly.

Legal Notice:

No modification, distribution, sale, use or quotation of the contents of this book is permitted without the express consent of the author.

Disclaimer Notice:

The information contained in this book is for educational and entertainment purposes only. No express or implied warranties of any kind are made. Readers acknowledge that the author is not offering legal, financial, medical or professional advice.

Index

VOLUME I

Understanding your emotions

Introduction to Volume I

Somewhere in the world, amidst the daily struggles and adversities that life throws at us, there are stories of strength, resilience and beauty that deserve to be told. These stories are ours.

"Emotional Empowerment and Inner Strength: A Black Woman's Guide to Emotional Self-Care" is a journey through emotions, self-discovery and empowerment.

This book is not just a set of words; it is meant to be a warm and comforting embrace for each of you who, like me, have faced challenges in our lives.

It is an in-depth exploration of what it means to be a black woman today, with all the lights and shadows that come with it.

In the chaotic landscape of modern life, we all face obstacles, challenges and emotions that often bewilder us. But for us black women, this journey is marked by unique struggles and experiences that shape us in profound and sometimes misunderstood ways.

We suffer from gender discrimination, but we also face racial discrimination. Our needs and voices are often ignored, and we simultaneously have our own responsibilities as mothers, daughters, friends, professionals and community members.

In this context, the question arises: How do we find inner peace and emotional empowerment to live an authentic and meaningful life? This book is an invitation to a transformative journey towards understanding and mastering our emotions.

We know that living in this skin means sailing in turbulent waters and facing strong winds, but it also means possessing a strength, grace and inner beauty that are truly unmatched.

This book is divided into two volumes, each designed to illuminate different aspects of your being. In the first volume, "Understanding Your Emotions", we will discover the root of our emotions, how they work, how they affect us and how we can harness their power for our benefit.

From demystifying emotions to challenging common distortions of thinking, this tome will give you the tools you need to confidently navigate the vast world of your feelings.

But the journey does not end here. In the second volume, "Cultivating Your Emotional Wellbeing", we will go even further in the practical application of your emotional understanding.

We will discover zen wisdom that can help us find inner peace in the midst of the emotional storm and learn strategies to maintain inner calm, release emotions in a constructive way and cultivate resilience in the midst of challenges.

I will give you strategies to release emotional build-up before your emotions overflow, and I will teach you how to channel that energy to be happier and move through life with a smile on your face. And you will rediscover joy and authenticity in your life, nurturing your inner peace and prioritizing your long-term well-being.

Throughout both volumes, you will find exercises and questions designed to help you connect with yourself, explore your emotions and move forward on a journey of self-discovery and self-care.

In addition, you'll find three valuable bonuses at the end of the book: self-care exercises, guidance on finding and creating a supportive community, and a complete guide to creating your own personalized self-care plan.

This book will guide you through your emotions, providing you with the tools and knowledge to find the inner peace, strength and happiness you deserve.

It's time to give yourself the gift of emotional self-care and discover the deep inner strength you've always had.

Get ready for a transformative journey towards emotional empowerment and wellness, and let's begin this journey together towards a more fulfilling and authentic life.

Chapter 1.

The Nature of Emotions

Emotions are a fundamental human component, from the elation of joy to the heaviness of sadness. Emotions are present in everyone's daily life and in particular of black women, as they forge an essential part of our identity and trajectory.

To fully understand emotions in the context of black women, it is essential to begin by demystifying some beliefs. Often, because of our race, we face stereotypes and expectations that require us to maintain constant strength in the midst of challenges and adversity.

The open expression of our emotions is sometimes interpreted as a weakness, which can lead to repressing feelings. However, it is essential to recognize that emotions are natural responses to experiences and situations; denying them is not a sign of strength but an act of denial of our own humanity.

Modern psychology has identified a wide range of emotions, and we experience these emotions in a unique context. The joy of achievement and resilience in the face of adversity are examples of emotions that play a prominent role in our lives. We often experience emotions such as anger and frustration related to the struggle against racial and gender discrimination, but we also feel the satisfaction of making significant progress.

Emotional communication is a crucial part of our lives. Expressing emotions through art, music and storytelling has been an important form of communication and resilience in the black community. Cultural expressions, such as soul music and blues, have been avenues for sharing deep emotions and a way to connect on an emotional level with others.

Emotions also have a substantial impact on our daily decisions and choices. The struggle for equality and justice is often driven by emotions such as determination and commitment. Understanding and embracing these emotions can be a powerful driver for activism and social change.

In addition to their influence on decisions, emotions also have an effect on our physical health and general well-being. Stress related to racial and gender discrimination can have a significant impact on our health, making emotional self-care an essential tool.

As you progress through this book, you will delve even deeper into the emotional world of black women and acquire tools to understand, manage and use their emotions effectively.

Emotions are automatic responses to internal or external stimuli. They are natural reactions and should not be judged as good or bad. Accepting our emotions and recognizing their existence is the first step towards understanding and emotional control.

Exercises and questions for reflection

<u>Exercise 1</u>

To better understand your emotions and how they affect you, take a few minutes to reflect on an emotion you have recently experienced. It can be an intense emotion or a more subtle one, but it should be a real emotional experience that you have lived through.

After recalling this emotion, answer the following questions:

1. What was the emotion you experienced? Describe this emotion in detail, including how it manifested in your body and mind.

   ____

   ____

   ____

   ____

   ____

2. Can you identify the trigger or situation that caused this emotion? If so, briefly describe it.

____

____

____

____

____

3. How did you initially react to this emotion? Did you try to repress it or did you accept it?

____

____

____

____

____

4. How did this emotion influence your thoughts and actions at the time?

____

____

____

____

____

5. What lessons can you learn from this emotional reflection? How could you apply this knowledge in future emotional situations?

____

____

____

____

____

Exercise 2

To better understand how emotions work, choose a specific emotion that you have recently experienced. It could be any emotion, either positive or negative.

Now, imagine this emotion as a cycle that begins, develops and finally fades away completely.

Answer the following questions about this experience:

1. Describe the emotion you selected for this exercise. How did you experience it in terms of intensity and duration?

   ____

   ____

   ____

   ____

   ____

2. What were the thoughts or situations that triggered this particular emotion?

   ____

   ____

   ____

   ____

   ____

3. While experiencing this emotion, what kinds of actions or behaviors did you perform or consider?

   ____

   ____

   ____

____

____

4. As the emotion faded, how did your thoughts and behaviors change? How did you feel afterwards?

____

____

____

____

____

5. Reflect on how understanding this emotional cycle might help you better manage this emotion in the future.

____

____

____

____

____

<u>Exercise 3</u>

Creativity can be a powerful tool to express and understand each of our emotions.

Choose an intense emotion that you have experienced in the past and use a form of creative expression, such as writing, painting, music or dance, to express that emotion.

Answer the following questions:

1. Why did you choose this particular emotion to express yourself creatively?

   ____

   ____

   ____

   ____

   ____

2. Describe the process of creative expression you used (e.g., writing a poem, painting a picture, creating a song). How did you feel while you were doing it?

____

____

____

____

____

3. What aspects of emotion can you express most clearly through your form of creative expression?

____

____

____

____

____

4. Was there anything surprising or revealing in the act of creatively expressing this emotion? Did you learn something new about yourself?

____

____

____

____

____

5. How did creative expression make you feel in terms of emotional release? Did you feel relieved?

____

____

____

____

____

Exercise 4

While having a conversation with another person, carefully observe their facial expression and body language and try to identify the emotions they may be experiencing.

As you practice this skill, answer the following questions:

1. Can you provide examples of facial expressions or body language cues that helped you identify the person's emotions?

____

____

____

____

____

2. How did you feel about being aware of the other person's emotions during the conversation? How do you think this skill could improve your relationships?

____

____

____

____

____

3. Did you ever notice if your own emotions responded to the other person's emotions during the conversation?

____

____

____

____

____

4. Was there ever a time when you found it difficult to identify the other person's emotions? What did you learn from that experience?

____

____

____

____

____

5. How could this ability to recognize emotions in others help you in your daily life and interpersonal relationships?

____

____

____

____

____

Exercise 5

Consciously choose an emotion and experience how it changes and evolves over a period of time.

You might choose an emotion that you would normally find challenging.

During this exercise, keep a record of your observations and emotional responses and then answer the following questions:

1. Which emotion do you choose for this exercise? Why?

   ____

   ____

   ____

   ____

   ____

2. Describe how you first felt when you experienced this emotion. How did it manifest in your body and mind?

____

____

____

____

____

3. Over the period of time, you chose, how did this emotion change? Were there times when they were more intense or less intense?

____

____

____

____

____

4. What thoughts or activities helped you maintain or change this emotion over time?

____

____

____

____

____

5. What conclusions can you draw about the nature of emotions from this exercise? How will this understanding help you in your daily life?

____

____

____

____

____

These exercises and questions will provide you with valuable tools to explore and understand your emotions in depth.

As you continue to work with these exercises, you will be on the path to greater emotional empowerment and a richer understanding of yourself.

1.1. Demystifying your emotions

Let's talk about something we often overlook: our emotions. We are convinced that we must be strong and brave at all times as if our emotions are a sign of weakness. But let me tell you something important: our emotions are a natural and valuable part of who we are.

Sometimes, we are told that showing emotions is a sign of vulnerability, but that is not true. Our emotions are like compasses that guide us through life. If you feel happy, sad, angry or any other emotion, it's okay. There are no "right" or "wrong" emotions. They are all part of our experience.

In psychology, many different emotions have been identified, all of which are relevant to us. Think of those times when you have felt joyful about your accomplishments or those times when you have felt angry about the injustices we face. These emotions are real and powerful, and we should not deny or repress them.

The way we communicate emotionally is unique and powerful. Often, we use art, music and our stories to express how we feel and connect with other black women. Soul and blues music, for example, have been a way to express the pain and joy of our community in a deep and beautiful way.

Our emotions also influence our decisions and actions. The determination we feel can drive us to fight for equality and justice. We must not be afraid of our emotions; we must learn to use them as tools for change and action.

In addition, our emotions affect our physical and mental health. The stress we face due to racial and gender discrimination can be overwhelming, so it is vital to take care of ourselves emotionally. Learning to manage and understand our emotions is an essential part of self-care.

Celebrate your emotions because they are a beautiful and valuable part of who you are.

1.2. How emotions affect your life

Since our experiences are unique and our emotions play a central role in all of this, let's now talk about how emotions impact our lives as black women.

Emotions are like waves in the ocean of our existence. They can be gentle and calm or powerful and tumultuous. But no matter how they feel, they profoundly affect every aspect of our lives.

First, our emotions influence our relationships. When we are happy, our smiles light up any room. But we also know how we feel when we are angry or frustrated, and that can affect our interactions with others.

It is critical to be aware of how our emotions impact our relationships and learn to communicate effectively, especially in a world that does not always understand our unique experiences.

Emotions also have an impact on our decisions. How many times have you felt a burning fire inside you when confronted with injustice or inequality? That anger can be a powerful engine for activism and social change.

But it is also important to remember that our emotions can influence our daily decisions, from how we spend our time to the choices we make at work or at home.

In addition, our emotions have a profound effect on our physical and mental health. Chronic stress related to racial and gender discrimination can be exhausting. Feeling anxious or overwhelmed can often have a negative impact on our well-being. Therefore, it is essential to take care of ourselves emotionally and learn strategies to manage stress.

We must not forget that our emotions are also a source of strength and resilience. The joy we feel when we celebrate our achievements and the determination that drives us to overcome obstacles are testaments to our resilience as black women.

Let us learn to accept our emotions as an integral part of who we are. Let us understand these powerful forces and learn to use them to empower ourselves and shape our lives in a meaningful way.

Always remember that your emotions are valid and beautiful. They are an essential part of your story and deserve to be understood and honored.

Chapter 2.

The Power of Self-Reflection

Let's talk about the powerful path to empowerment through self-reflection. Self-reflection is like looking into an emotional mirror, an intimate space where we can connect with our deepest feelings and discover emotional experiences that we may have kept deep in our hearts.

As a black woman, I know firsthand that we often face challenges that other people don't, and in the midst of it all, our emotions can be a difficult thing to understand and manage. But let me tell you, self-reflection can be the compass that guides us and helps us take back our power.

The first step toward self-reflection is learning to connect with our feelings. It may sound simple, but in reality, it is an act of courage. In a world that sometimes pressures us to be strong and stay calm at all times, stopping to feel our emotions can seem like a revolutionary act.

But here's the truth: our emotions are ours, and they have a purpose. When we take the time to connect with our feelings, we are honoring our humanity and experience.

To do this, we can start by asking ourselves simple questions: How do I feel today? Why do I feel the way I feel? Is there something that worries me or cheers me up? These questions are like a flashlight in the darkness of your emotions, illuminating the corners we may have avoided exploring.

As you delve deeper into this self-reflection, you will be surprised at how many emotional experiences you can discover. Perhaps you remember moments from your childhood or past events that still affect your life today. Or you may become aware of recurring emotional patterns that influence your relationships and decisions.

Some emotions can be painful, such as sadness or anger. Others can be a source of joy and gratitude, regardless of the feelings they are associated with; all of these emotions are part of you, and all deserve to be explored and understood.

Self-reflection also allows you to empower yourself and take control of your life. As you better understand your emotions and experiences, you can make decisions that are more aligned with your values and goals. You can heal old wounds and make room for personal growth.

I can't deny that self-reflection can be a challenging journey, but it is a worthwhile one. It helps you reclaim your power and live authentically.

Find time for yourself, give yourself permission to feel and explore the depths of your emotions. The power of self-reflection is waiting for you, and I am here to accompany you on this journey.

Exercises and questions for reflection

In our journey towards emotional empowerment, we have explored the importance of connecting with our emotions and discovering the emotional experiences that shape our lives.

Let us now begin this powerful process; let us learn to practice self-reflection in a more concrete way.

For this, I propose 5 new exercises; give yourself some time to reflect and answer each of the questions, and this will be very valuable to explore your emotions in a more meaningful way.

<u>Exercise 1</u>

Let's start with a simple but effective exercise: an emotion journal. This journal will be your companion on the journey of self-reflection. Here is a step-by-step guide:

- Find a notebook or an app to keep track. Choose a place where you feel comfortable and have a moment with your thoughts and feelings.

- Set a time. Set aside a time during the day to write in your emotion journal.
- Record your emotions. In each entry, start writing how you feel at that moment. Use words that describe your emotions, such as "happy," "sad," "frustrated," "grateful," or whatever you feel.
- Dig deeper into your emotions. After recording your main emotion, take some time to identify why you feel the way you do. Was there something specific that triggered that emotion? Does it remind you of a past experience?
- Reflect and close. Conclude each entry in your emotion journal with a brief reflection on what you have learned from connecting with your feelings, whether it is a note of encouragement to yourself or an intention for the day ahead.

Below is a series of questions that can serve as a guide for the development of this exercise:

1. What emotions are you experiencing today?

   ____

   ____

   ____

   ____

   ____

2. Were there any common patterns or triggers in your emotions?

   ____

   ____

   ____

   ____

   ____

3. How do you feel about delving into your emotions?

   ____

   ____

   ____

____

____

4. Did you discover any past emotional experiences that influence your current emotional state?

____

____

____

____

____

5. How do you feel after completing this exercise?

____

____

____

____

____

Exercise 2

Write a letter to your younger self. You can choose a particular age, such as your childhood or adolescence. In the letter, share your current emotions and the wisdom you have gained over time. This letter is an opportunity to connect with your past experiences and give you love and support.

1. At what age did you write the letter?

2. What emotions do you share in the letter?

3. What wisdom or advice would you give to your younger self?

____

____

4. How did writing this letter make you feel?

____

____

____

____

____

5. What would you like to tell your future self?

____

____

____

____

____

Exercise 3

Explore your emotions in a creative and visual way by following these steps:

- Gather your materials. Look for old magazines or newspapers and gather scissors, glue and a large surface to work on.

- Explore emotions. Leaf through magazines, and look for pictures, images or words that represent your current or past emotions. They can be facial expressions, landscapes, colors or key words.

- Create your collage. Cut out the images and words you have selected and paste them on the cardboard or paper in a creative way. Don't worry about the layout; just follow your intuition.

- Reflect on your collage. After completing your collage of emotions, sit in front of it and look at what you have created. What emotions do you see represented? Are you surprised by any particular image or word? How does the collage as a whole make you feel?

Complete the exercise by answering the following questions:

1. What emotions did you choose to represent in your collage?

____

____

____

____

____

2. Were there any images or words that surprised you or particularly resonated with you?

____

____

____

____

____

3. How did the creation of this collage make you feel?

____

____

____

____

____

4. What patterns or themes do you observe in your collage?

____

____

____

____

5. How can you use this creative experience to connect more deeply with your emotions in everyday life?

____

____

____

____

<u>Exercise 4</u>

This exercise involves a person close to you, such as a trusted friend or family member.

The idea is to have an honest conversation about emotions.

You can do it in the following way:

- Choose your interview partner. Find someone with whom you feel comfortable and safe to talk about your emotions.
- Prepare some questions. Think of open-ended questions that will help you explore your emotions. For example, "How are you feeling today?", "What emotions have you experienced recently?" or "When do you feel most connected to yourself emotionally?".
- Share and listen. Take turns asking and answering questions. Encourage your interview partner to share his or her emotions

as well. The key here is understanding and mutual empathy.

- Reflect after the conversation. Take some time to reflect on what you learned. Were there any emotions you hadn't explored before? How did it make you feel to talk about your emotions with someone you trust?

Now answer the following questions related to the exercise:

1. How did you feel about sharing your emotions with your interview partner?

____

____

____

____

____

2. Were there any new or profound emotions that you discovered during the conversation?

____

____

____

____

____

3. What did you feel when you heard your partner's emotions?

____

____

____

____

____

4. What did you learn from this emotion interview experience?

____

____

____

____

____

5. How would you apply what you have learned in your daily life to better connect with yourself emotionally?

Exercise 5

For this last exercise, you will need paper and colored pencils or markers. The idea is to represent your emotions through art. Follow these steps:

- Gather your materials: paper and drawing tools, such as colored pencils or markers.
- Choose an emotion. Think of an emotion you want to explore through art. It can be happiness, sadness, anger, calmness, or whatever you are feeling at the time.
- Draw your emotion. Use the colors and shapes to represent the emotion you chose.
- Reflect on your drawing. After completing your artwork, look at it carefully. What

symbol for you? How does it make you feel to see your emotion captured on paper?

Then answer the following questions about the previous exercise:

1. What emotion did you choose to represent in your drawing?

____

____

____

____

____

2. What colors and shapes do you use to express that emotion?

____

____

____

____

____

3. How did drawing your emotion make you feel?

____

____

____

____

____

4. What symbolism do you find in your emotional artwork?

____

____

____

____

____

5. How do you feel after creating this emotional drawing?

____

____

____

____

____

These five exercises are designed to help you deepen your self-reflection. Each one gives you the opportunity to connect with yourself on a deeper level and better understand your feelings.

As you progress in self-reflection, you will find a strong sense of empowerment and self-knowledge.

2.1. Connect with your feelings

When I talk about "connecting with your feelings", I don't just mean having them, but truly experiencing them, discovering their richness and depth. Your emotions are a gift, a valuable part of who you are and you deserve to be honored.

You may have been told that you should be strong at all times and that you should not show vulnerability. But I want you to understand that showing your emotions is not a sign of weakness.

Every tear shed and every laugh released are manifestations of your inner strength and your ability to live authentically.

Connecting with your feelings is like opening the door to your heart. It can be scary at first, especially if you've been used to keeping your emotions silent. But I assure you it is a liberating act.

It allows you to understand yourself on a deeper level and gives you the clarity to make decisions aligned with your values and desires.

Here are some ways to start connecting with your feelings:

1. Allow yourself to feel. When an emotion arises, don't repress it. Allow yourself to feel it fully, without judgment. Emotions are messengers, and each one has something important to tell you.

2. Explore your emotional patterns. Ask yourself if there are recurring patterns in your emotions: Do you often feel anger? Do you experience joy in certain situations? Knowing your emotional patterns will help you understand your reactions to various circumstances.

3. Talk about your emotions. Sharing your feelings with trusted friends or counselors can be very freeing. Sometimes, expressing what you are feeling out loud helps you process those emotions in a deeper way.

4. Practice self-reflection. Take time for yourself and do this on a regular basis, whether through meditation, journaling or simply sitting in silence. This time will allow you to connect with yourself and explore your deepest emotions.

5. Celebrate your emotions. Enjoy the diversity of your feelings, even those that may be difficult. They are all expressions of your humanity.

As black women, our experiences may be unique, but our emotions are a bridge that connects us. By connecting with our feelings and sharing this journey, we strengthen our community and empower each other.

So, sister, I encourage you not to be afraid to feel, to explore and to embrace every aspect of yourself. In your emotions, you will find a source of power and authenticity that will guide you on your journey to wholeness and empowerment.

2.2. Discovering your emotional experiences

Now, I want to talk to you about how to discover your emotional experiences. As black women, our lives are filled with unique experiences, rich in nuance and color. Every emotion we experience is a part of our beautiful story.

Our emotions are complex and carry with them a piece of our history. It may be the joy of a personal achievement, sadness at the injustices we face, or the satisfaction of overcoming seemingly insurmountable obstacles.

Often, our emotions echo the experiences we have lived through as black women in a world that has sometimes denied us empathy and understanding.

To discover our own emotional experiences, it is important that we practice self-reflection and look inward, review our experiences and discover how they have shaped us.

Some ways to begin this journey are:

- Keeping an emotional diary.
- Recall key moments in your life that have had an emotional impact. Do you remember how you felt at the time? What did you learn from those experiences?
- Talking and sharing your emotional experiences with other black women can provide valuable insight and meaningful connections. Together, we can learn and grow!

Our emotions are powerful guides. Every emotion we experience carries a message, a lesson or a revelation:

- Anger can be a sign that something is out of place and needs to be changed.
- Joy can be a reminder of beauty and gratitude for what we have.

- Sadness can be a healing and liberating process.

As we explore our emotional experiences, we must remember that there are no "wrong" emotions. Each is valid and deserves to be understood.

By recognizing our emotions, we are recognizing our own humanity.

Questions for Self-Reflection:

- What are some of the most powerful emotional experiences you have had as a black woman?
- How have you learned from your emotions throughout your life?
- What emotions challenged or inspired you the most?
- How have your emotional experiences influenced your decisions and choices in life?
- What steps can you take to explore and understand your emotions more deeply?

Self-reflection is an invitation to know yourself more deeply, to celebrate your emotions and to empower yourself through self-knowledge. Your emotional experiences are an essential part of your story and deserve to be honored. On this path, you will find a greater understanding of yourself and a greater connection to your Black women's community.

Chapter 3.

Origin of Emotional Responses

I want to talk to you about the origin of our emotional responses. Understanding the origin of our emotional responses is a fundamental step on the path to emotional empowerment and self-acceptance.

For this, the first thing we need to know are the triggers, i.e. events, situations or words that provoke an emotional response in us. Often, these triggers come from our past experiences. They can be memories of painful or challenging moments, or a response to the stresses and expectations we face in our daily lives.

Our triggers are personal and unique to each of us, so what may trigger a strong emotional response in one person may not have the same effect on another.

Our triggers are shaped by our experiences and the way we perceive the world around us.

Now, once we recognize our triggers, the next step is to learn to manage our emotional responses. We cannot completely control what triggers us, but we can control how we respond to those emotions and for this, there are strategies, some of which can help us in this process:

- Practice self-awareness. Learn to identify your emotional triggers. Ask yourself, "What made me feel this way?" Taking a moment to reflect on your emotions can help you understand them better.
- Take a few deep breaths. When faced with an intense emotional response, take a few deep breaths. Mindful breathing can help you calm down and maintain mental clarity.
- Talk about your emotions. Sharing what you are feeling with close friends or trusted counselors can be therapeutic. Sometimes, putting your emotions into words can ease the intensity of the emotional response.

- Find healthy ways to release emotions. Exercise, meditation and creativity can be effective ways to release pent-up emotional energy. Find activities that will help you process your emotions in a healthy way.
- Practice self-care. Take care of yourself and your emotional well-being. Self-care is a crucial part of maintaining strong emotional health.
- Reflect, try to ask yourself questions and answer: Can you identify some of the emotional triggers in your life? How have you learned to manage your emotional responses over the years? Are there specific strategies that will help you calm down when faced with an intense emotional response? What ways of releasing emotions do you find most effective and satisfying? How can you incorporate emotional self-care into your daily routine?

Recognizing the source of our emotional responses is a fundamental step in achieving emotional empowerment. As we explore our experiences and learn to manage our emotions, we become stronger and move closer to a greater understanding of ourselves.

Exercises and questions for reflection

<u>Exercise 1</u>

1. Can you think of a recent situation in which you experienced an intense emotional response? What triggered that emotion?

   ____

   ____

   ____

   ____

   ____

2. How did you become aware that you were experiencing an emotional response? Were there physical or emotional signs indicating this?

   ____

   ____

____

____

____

3. How do you manage your many emotional responses? Do you allow yourself to feel and process your emotions or do you tend to repress them?

____

____

____

____

____

4. Are there recurring patterns in your emotional triggers? Have you noticed that certain situations or words tend to elicit similar responses in you?

____

____

____

____

____

5. Reflect on how you feel after identifying your emotional triggers. Do you feel more empowered to manage your emotions?

____

____

____

____

____

Exercise 2

Think of an emotional response that you have found difficult to handle in the past.

1. What strategies or tools do you use to manage that emotion?

____

____

____

____

____

2. Have you found any specific technique that helps you calm down when you experience an intense emotional response? If so, what is it?

____

____

____

____

____

3. Have you ever shared your emotional responses with close friends or trusted advisors? How has that experience helped you?

____

____

____

____

____

4. What activities or hobbies do you find most effective in releasing pent-up emotions and maintaining your emotional balance?

____

____

____

____

____

5. What plans do you have to incorporate emotional self-care into your daily routine? How will you ensure that you prioritize your emotional well-being?

____

____

____

____

____

<u>Exercise 3</u>

Think of an emotionally significant experience from your past.

1. How did you feel? How do you feel remembering her?

____

____

____

____

____

2. What have you learned from that past emotional experience and how has it influenced your current perceptions and decisions?

____

____

____

____

____

3. Have you ever shared this emotional experience with other black women who may have had similar experiences? What was that conversation like?

____

____

____

____

____

4. What steps can you take to honor and celebrate your past emotional experiences, even if they were challenging?

____

____

____

____

____

5. Reflect on how you feel after exploring your past emotional experiences. Do you feel that you have gained a greater understanding of yourself and your history?

____

____

____

____

____

<u>Exercise 4</u>

Read the following questions, remember, reflect, analyze and answer each of them in the spaces provided.

1. Have you ever experienced emotional release through art, music, photography, dance, singing or storytelling? How has this form of emotional communication helped you?

   ____

   ____

   ____

   ____

   ____

2. Can you think of a song, movie or work of art that has reflected your emotions or experiences as a black woman? How did that artistic expression make you feel?

   ____

   ____

   ____

____

____

3. Have you shared your emotional experiences through art? How has it allowed you to connect with others?

____

____

____

____

____

4. What forms of emotional communication do you consider have been most liberating and most effective in your life?

____

____

____

____

____

5. How do you plan to incorporate more artistic and emotional expression into your daily life?

____

____

____

____

____

<u>Exercise 5</u>

Think of an important decision you have made in your life.

1. How did your emotions influence your decision? Was it a conscious or impulsive choice?

____

____

____

____

____

2. Have you ever found yourself in a situation where your emotional intuition led you to make the right decision?

____

____

____

____

____

3. How do you think you could use your emotions as a guide in future decisions? What steps can you take to make decisions that are more conscious and aligned with your emotional values?

____

____

____

____

____

4. Have you noticed how social expectations or stigma can influence your emotional decisions? How can you challenge these influences and make authentic choices?

____

____

____

____

____

5. Are you connected to your emotional intuition and better able to make authentic decisions?

____

____

____

____

____

This chapter is an essential step toward emotional empowerment. By exploring and understanding our emotional responses, our triggers and how we manage our emotions, we are strengthening ourselves and growing in our ability to live more authentic and fulfilling lives as Black women.

Your story and emotions are valuable and deserve to be explored and honored. Together, we can support each other on this path to self-awareness and emotional resilience.

3.1. Identifying triggers

Let's talk about something that, as black women, we sometimes face without even realizing it: emotional triggers. They are like those stones in the road that trip us up, but by understanding them, we can learn to navigate them with grace.

Triggers are the sparks that ignite our emotions. They can be words, situations or even looks that affect us deeply. It is important to recognize that each of us has our own triggers. What may affect one in a certain way may not affect another.

Triggers can be memories of difficult times, discrimination or challenges we have faced. They may also be linked to the expectations society has of us as black women.

How to identify your triggers?

- Self-observation: Pay attention to how you feel in various situations. When do you feel particularly emotional? What led you to feel that way?

- Physical reactions: Your body also gives you clues about your triggers. Does your heart beat faster? Do you feel tension in your muscles? These reactions can indicate that you're dealing with a trigger.

- Record your experiences: Keeping an emotional journal can be helpful. Write down situations that have affected you emotionally and how you felt. Over time, you will be able to detect patterns.

- Share with friends: Talking with other black women can be eye-opening. Sharing your experiences and hearing about others' experiences can help you identify common triggers.

- Seek professional help: In some cases, it may be helpful to attend therapy or seek the support of a specialist or counselor to help you explore and identify what your triggers are in a much deeper way.

Questions for Reflection:

- Can you identify an emotional trigger that has recently arisen in your life?
- How did you become aware that you were experiencing an emotional response to that trigger?
- Have you noticed recurring patterns in your emotional triggers? What similar types of situations tend to elicit responses?
- What physical reactions do you experience when faced with an emotional trigger?
- How do you feel about becoming aware of your triggers? Do you think this knowledge can help you manage your emotions more effectively?

Identifying our triggers is important to achieve emotional empowerment. It helps us understand why we react in certain ways and gives us the opportunity to make conscious decisions about how we want to handle those emotions.

3.2. Managing Emotional Responses

Sometimes, our emotions can feel like an endless roller coaster. But here we are, ready to learn how to manage those emotional responses and become empowered.

When an emotion invades you, do not forget that you are strong and resilient, and that you can also use strategies to manage them, some of them are:

- Take deep breaths: Taking a moment to breathe deeply can help you calm down.
- Talk to someone you trust: Find a friend you trust and share what is affecting you.
- Practice self-care: This is not a selfish attitude; it's a necessity. Whether it's a relaxing bath, a walk in nature or listening to

your favorite music, find ways to take care of yourself.

- Meditation and *mindfulness*: These practices help you to be present in the moment and observe your emotions without judgment.

- Therapy: If you feel that emotions often get the best of you, consider seeking the help of a therapist. They can provide you with tools and support to navigate your emotions in a healthy way.

Questions for Reflection

- What strategies do you use to calm yourself when you experience an intense emotional response?

- Have you ever shared your emotional responses with trusted friends? How has that experience helped you?

- What activities or hobbies do you find most effective in releasing pent-up emotions and maintaining your emotional balance?

- How do you make sure you incorporate emotional self-care into your daily routine?
- What do you plan to do to manage your emotions more effectively in the future?

Managing our emotional responses is an act of self-love and strength. We do not have to be prisoners of our emotions; we can be their drivers.

Chapter 4.

Body and Mind: Emotional Bonding

Let me tell you about a deep and powerful connection: the relationship between our body and our mind. The two are intertwined in a constant dance. What we feel emotionally can manifest in our body and vice versa. This means that, in order to take care of our emotions, we must pay attention to our bodies and vice versa.

When you are stressed, your body may respond with muscle tension, insomnia or headaches, and when you feel happy and relaxed, your body may respond with a sense of lightness and well-being. This deep connection between body and mind shows us that we cannot address our emotions without considering our physical well-being.

Now, how do we balance this relationship between body and mind? Here are some practices that can help you:

- *Mindfulness* practice: Take time to be present with your body and mind. Meditation and *mindfulness* allow you to observe your thoughts and bodily sensations without judgment. This can help you become more aware of your emotions and manage them effectively.

- Regular Exercise: Exercise not only benefits your body but also your mind. The release of endorphins during exercise can improve your mood and reduce stress.

- Self-care: Take time to relax with any activity that makes you feel good about yourself.

- Healthy Nutrition: What you put in your body can influence your emotions. Nutritious foods can keep your energy levels stable and improve your emotional well-being.

- Body Therapy: Consider therapies such as massage or acupuncture to release physical and emotional tensions stored in the body.

By taking care of both our bodies and our minds, we move closer to a more balanced and fulfilling life.

We are strong and resilient, and this connection helps us remember how powerful we are.

Exercises and questions for reflection

<u>Exercise 1</u>: *Mindfulness* Practice

- Find a quiet place where you can sit or lie down comfortably.
- Close your eyes and begin to pay attention to your breathing. Feel how the air enters and leaves your body.
- As you inhale and exhale, direct your attention to the sensations in your body. Is there any tension or discomfort anywhere?
- Let your thoughts flow, but don't get attached to them. Simply observe your thoughts as clouds passing through the sky of your mind.
- Continue this practice for at least 10 minutes.
1. How did it feel to practice *mindfulness*?

____

____

____

____

____

2. Were you able to notice any tension or discomfort in your body during the practice?

____

____

____

____

____

3. What thoughts came up as you meditated? How did you handle them?

____

____

____

____

4. Do you think mindfulness could be beneficial to you in your daily life?

____

____

____

____

____

5. What did you learn about yourself through mindfulness?

____

____

____

____

____

Exercise 2

Regular Exercise

- Choose a physical activity that you enjoy, whether it is walking, swimming, dancing, etc.
- Dedicate at least 30 minutes a day to this activity for a week.
- Keep track of how you feel emotionally before and after each exercise session.

Reflect on how the physical exercise influenced your emotional well-being at the end of the week.

1. How do you feel about your regular exercise routine?

____

____

____

____

____

2. Do you notice changes in your mood before and after exercise?

____

____

____

____

3. How did the physical exercise make you feel emotionally?

____

____

____

____

____

4. Do you think regular exercise could be an effective way to manage your emotions?

____

____

____

____

____

5. What conclusions did you draw from your week of exercise and emotion logging?

____

____

____

____

____

Exercise 3

Self-care

- Spend an afternoon or a whole day taking care of yourself.
- Plan activities that make you feel good about yourself, whether it's a relaxing bath, reading a good book, watching a movie or doing a creative activity.
- As you do these activities, pay attention to how you feel emotionally.
- At the end of the day, reflect on how self-care impacted your emotions.

1. How did it make you feel to take time to take care of yourself?

____

____

____

____

____

2. Do you notice any changes in your emotional state?

____

____

____

____

____

3. Which self-care activity impacted you the most?

____

____

____

____

____

4. Do you believe that self-care is an important part of your emotional well-being?

____

____

____

____

____

5. What lessons did you take away from your self-care day regarding your emotions?

____

____

____

____

____

Exercise 4

Body-Mind Connection

- Find a quiet place where you can be alone for a few minutes. Close your eyes and pay attention to your body. Can you feel any tension or discomfort in any part of your body? Observe it without judgment.
- Bring your attention to your breathing. Inhale deeply through your nose, feeling the air fill your lungs, and exhale slowly through your mouth. Do this several times to calm your mind.
- When you are more relaxed, think of a recent situation that has generated an intense emotion

in you, either positive or negative. Try to relive it in your mind and pay attention to the sensations you experience in your body as you do so.

- After a couple of minutes, stop the visualization and refocus on your breathing. Inhaling and exhaling, try to release any tension accumulated during this activity.

1. What physical sensations did you experience when you thought about the emotionally charged situation?

____

____

____

____

____

2. Was there any part of your body that showed obvious signs of tension or discomfort?

____

____

____

____

____

3. How did it feel to focus on your breath and release that tension?

____

____

____

____

____

4. Do you think this mind-body connection practice could be helpful in situations where you feel emotionally overwhelmed?

____

____

____

____

____

5. Did I ask you in any way how your body reacted to your thoughts and emotions?

____

____

____

____

____

Exercise 5

Emotional Writing

- Take a few minutes to write about a recent emotional experience you have had. You can choose a positive or negative experience, whichever makes you feel more comfortable.

- Write down everything you feel about that experience. Let your emotions flow. What feelings come over you? Where do you feel those emotions?

- When you finish reading what you have written, what patterns emerge from your words? Is there a relationship between your emotions and the sensations in your body?

1. How did it feel to write about your emotional experience? Did you find it liberating or challenging?

   ____

   ____

   ____

   ____

   ____

2. Were you able to identify any connection between your emotions and the physical sensations in your body while writing?

   ____

   ____

   ____

   ____

   ____

3. What patterns or themes did you notice in your words? Were you surprised by any revelations during this exercise?

____

____

____

____

____

4. Do you think emotional writing could become a useful tool for understanding and managing your emotions in the future?

____

____

____

____

____

5. What has this exercise taught you about the relationship between your body and your emotions?

____

____

____

I hope these exercises and questions help you. Exploring the mind-body connection is a step towards emotional empowerment.

4.1. The body - mind connection

Let's talk about the powerful connection between our body and mind, a relationship we often overlook in our quest for strength and endurance.

From the moment we wake up in the morning, our bodies and minds are intertwined. Our thoughts, emotions and experiences profoundly affect the way our body feels and responds, and vice versa. This connection is not a weakness; it is a strength that we must learn to use to our advantage.

As black women, when faced with racial and gender discrimination, it is common for us to feel overwhelmed. Anger, frustration and sadness can become constant companions on our journey.

But it is important to remember that these emotions do not only exist in our minds; we also feel them in our bodies. It is that tension in the shoulders, the knot in the stomach or the acceleration of the heart; all these are signs that our emotions are essentially affecting our being.

But here's the beauty of this connection: if we can learn to listen to and understand our body's signals, we can influence our emotions in a positive way.

Practicing *mindfulness* allows us to tune into our physical and emotional sensations. When we take a moment to breathe deeply and notice where our emotions manifest in our bodies, we gain a greater awareness of what is happening inside us.

In addition, we can use exercise as a powerful tool. When we move and take care of our bodies, we release endorphins that can improve our mood and relieve stress. It's not just a matter of physical appearance; it's about empowering our minds through physical activity.

This mind-body connection should not forget that self-reflection is an ally. By writing about our emotional and bodily experiences, we can discover patterns and triggers that will help us better navigate our emotions.

Understanding that our body and mind are one is a vital step towards emotional self-care. It is not about separating our emotions from our physical being but embracing the wholeness of who we are and using this connection to strengthen us on our journey.

4.2. Exercises to balance your emotions

Let's talk about exercises to balance our emotions, a valuable tool for our emotional empowerment. These exercises can help us heal, strengthen and navigate the often turbulent waters of our lives with grace.

What are the Emotion Balancing Exercises?

Emotional balancing exercises are practices that engage our mind and body to help us better manage and understand our emotions. These exercises can be simple or more elaborate, but their main purpose is to help us find inner peace and emotional stability.

What are they for?

These emotional self-care tools serve to:

- Stress management: It helps us to release accumulated tension and find calm in times of agitation.
- Encourage self-reflection: They allow us to explore our emotions and better understand what we feel and why we feel it.
- Promote resilience: Strengthen our ability to face challenges and adversity with grace and endurance.
- Cultivate gratitude and positivity: They help us focus on the positive in our lives, even when we face challenges.

Why are they important to us?

Emotional balancing exercises are especially important for us black women for several reasons:

- Emotional empowerment: Helps us take control of our emotions and no longer let stereotypes or discrimination tell us how we should feel.
- Mental health: They can contribute to our mental health by reducing stress and promoting self-reflection.
- Resilience: By strengthening our emotional resilience, we become more capable of facing challenges and moving forward, even in the face of adversity.

Benefits of Practicing Emotion Balancing Exercises:

- Stress and anxiety reduction.
- Greater mental clarity.
- Increased emotional self-awareness.
- Promotion of self-reflection and self-knowledge.
- Increased emotional resilience.

- Increased ability to deal with challenges and conflicts.

Who can make them?

We can all do them! It doesn't matter your age, gender or life situation. Emotional balancing exercises are for all of us, no matter where we come from or where we are going.

Types of Exercises

There are several types of exercises to balance emotions, such as:

- Breathing exercises: These help calm the mind and body, such as deep breathing and mindfulness.

- Gratitude practices: Focusing on the positive in our lives and recognizing blessings.

- Physical exercise: Physical activity releases endorphins that improve mood and relieve stress.

- Meditation and *mindfulness*: These practices help us to be present and manage stress.

- Therapeutic writing: Keeping a journal of emotions or writing about experiences can be very healing.
- Relaxation techniques: such as yoga or gentle stretching.

But let's talk about some specific exercises that can help us, as black women, balance our emotions and strengthen our mind-body connection.

These exercises are wonderful, as they are designed to help us find that space of calm and resilience that we need and are looking for in the midst of the many daily struggles we face.

Exercise 1: Conscious Breathing. Close your eyes and sit in a quiet place. Begin to pay attention to your breathing. Inhale deeply through your nose, feeling your abdomen expand. Then, exhale slowly through your mouth. Do this for a few minutes.

As you practice this mindful breathing, visualize that you inhale calm and strength and exhale tension and worry. This will help you balance your emotions and find a space of tranquility within.

Exercise 2: Gratitude Ritual. Spend a few minutes each day writing down three things you are grateful for. It can be something big or small, like the support of a loved one or the sun shining outside. This exercise will help you focus on the positive, even in the midst of challenges.

Exercise 3: Yoga or Stretching. Yoga and gentle stretches are a powerful way to connect with your body and release emotional tension. It's not about doing perfect poses but about moving your body with love and care. There are many free online classes you can try from the comfort of your home.

Exercise 4: Emotion Journal. Keep an emotion journal. Write down your feelings and thoughts every day. This will help you track emotional patterns and better understand how different situations affect you.

Exercise 5: Self-Compassion Practice. Close your eyes and place a hand on your heart. Repeat self-compassionate affirmations, such as "I deserve love and care" or "I am strong and resilient." This simple gesture can help you connect with yourself and cultivate a more compassionate relationship with yourself.

Questions for Reflection:

- How do you feel when practicing these exercises?
- Do you notice any changes in your emotional state after doing them regularly?
- Which of these exercises did you find most helpful in your search for emotional balance?
- How do you plan to incorporate these exercises into your daily routine?
- What have you learned about yourself through these exercises?

In our search for emotional balance, we can choose the exercises that resonate most with us and suit our needs.

Remember that emotional balance is a journey, and each small step brings us closer to the inner peace and resilience we seek.

Chapter 5.

Challenging Distortions in Thinking

Thought distortions are those negative or irrational ideas that sometimes take over our minds, making us feel bad about ourselves and limiting our potential.

As black women, we face unique challenges, and these distortions can be even more detrimental to us. But we can learn to challenge them and develop healthier, more positive thinking.

First of all, it is essential to recognize that there are several types of thought distortions that can affect us; some of the most common are: Catastrophic thinking, Polarization, Mental filtering, Personalization, Labeling and Unfounded Assumptions.

After knowing what the common distortions are, we can use strategies to change them into healthier thoughts, such as:

- Look for real evidence to support our thoughts
- Practicing gratitude
- Challenging catastrophic thinking
- Avoiding polarization
- Speak to yourself with kindness; don't judge yourself.
- Practicing *Mindfulness*

By having healthy thoughts, we will gain many benefits, as it is an act of self-love, self-esteem and empowerment. By challenging thought distortions, we can achieve:

- Increased self-esteem, security and we will feel better about ourselves.
- Reduce stress, negativity and self-criticism.
- Make more conscious decisions based on reality rather than assumptions.
- Improve our relationships and interactions with others.
- Greater resistance to adversity.
- Greater capacity and courage to face challenges.

Our thoughts are powerful. We can challenge thought distortions, change to healthy thoughts and have peace of mind. We deserve loving and positive thoughts.

Here are 5 exercises designed to help you go deeper about your emotions and foster greater emotional understanding and authenticity. Take the time to analyze and reflect on your responses:

Exercises and questions for reflection

Exercise 1

Exploring emotions through music

Choose a song that transmits emotions to you. Listen to it carefully, and identify what you are feeling as you listen to it. Then, write down your thoughts and feelings in response to the music.

1. Why did you choose this particular song?

____

____

____

____

____

2. What emotions do you experience while listening to the music?

____

____

____

____

____

3. Was there a specific moment in the song that made an emotional impact on you?

____

____

____

____

4. How did you feel about expressing your emotions through writing?

____

____

____

____

____

5. Do you think this practice can help you connect more deeply with your emotions through music?

____

____

____

____

____

Exercise 2

Visualization of emotions

Close your eyes and visualize a situation that has provoked intense emotion in the past. Relive the scene in your mind and pay attention to the emotions that arise. Then, imagine how you might have responded differently to manage those emotions more effectively.

1. Which situation do you choose for visualization and why?

____

____

____

____

____

2. What emotions did you relive during the
visualization?

____

____

____

____

____

3. How did it feel to imagine a different answer?

____

____

____

____

4. What lessons can you draw from this practice in
relation to emotion management?

____

____

____

____

____

5. How can you apply these learnings in future situations?

____

____

____

____

____

<u>Exercise 3</u>

Emotions in nature

- Spend time outdoors and connect with nature.
- Observe the environment around you and take note of how you feel in that space and what feelings it inspires in you.

- Reflect on how nature reflects your emotions and inner processes.

1. What aspects of nature caught your attention?

____

____

____

____

____

2. What emotions did you experience in nature?

____

____

____

____

3. Can you identify any similarities between your emotional state and what you observe in nature?

____

____

____

____

____

4. How do you feel about connecting with the beauty and tranquility of nature?

____

____

____

____

____

5. How can you integrate this connection to nature into your daily life to support your emotional well-being?

____

____

____

____

____

<u>Exercise 4</u>

Emotional dialogue

Imagine you can have a conversation with an emotion. Write a dialogue between the two, analyzing your thoughts and feelings towards it.

1. What emotion did you choose for the dialogue and why?

   ____

   ____

   ____

   ____

   ____

2. What would you like to tell him and hear in response?

   ____

   ____

   ____

   ____

   ____

3. How did you feel about writing the emotional dialogue?

____

____

____

____

____

4. Did you discover any new perspective or understand that emotion through the exercise?

____

____

____

____

____

5. How can you apply this emotional dialogue technique in your life and manage your emotions?

____

____

____

____

____

<u>Exercise 5</u>

Emotional collage

Create a visual collage that represents your current emotions. Cut out images from magazines, photos or drawn elements that symbolize them.

Look at your collage and reflect on what it reveals about your emotional world at this moment.

1. What elements do you include in your collage and why?

____

____

____

____

____

2. What emotions does your collage represent?

____

____

____

____

____

3. How did you feel during the creation process?

____

____

____

____

____

4. What new perspectives do you have when looking at your final collage?

____

____

____

____

____

5. How can you use this emotional collage technique to further discover and analyze your emotions in the future?

5.1. Recognizing common distortions

Let's talk about the most common thinking distortions we have. It is essential to recognize and challenge them as they can cloud our perception and limit our growth.

Distortions are thought patterns that lead us to see reality in a distorted way, usually in a negative way.

It's those voices in our head that sometimes tell us we're not good enough, that we're destined to fail or that no one values us.

Often, these distortions have come to us because of our past experiences or because of the expectations that society or we ourselves have imposed on ourselves.

Some of the common distortions we black women face include:

- Catastrophic thinking: Occurs when we anticipate the worst in any situation. For example, when we think that we will never be promoted because of an ill-intentioned comment at work.

- Polarization: When we see things in black and white without nuance. We may feel either that we are doing everything right or everything wrong, with no middle ground.

- Mental filtering: We focus only on the negative aspects of a situation, which leads us to constantly feel dissatisfied.

- Personalization: Self-blaming ourselves for everything bad that happens around us. For example, thinking that the discrimination we face is our fault.

- Labeling: Labeling ourselves negatively for past mistakes affects our self-esteem and self-image.

- Unfounded assumptions: Making assumptions without real evidence. For example, assuming that someone does not love us without concrete evidence.

- Overgeneralization: Occurs when we take one negative experience and apply it to all areas of our life. For example, if we face discrimination in one context, and we believe that we will always be treated unfairly in all aspects of our lives.

- Magnification of the negative: When we focus on the negative and minimize the positive.

- Victim mentality: When we feel trapped in the role of victim, it prevents us from taking control of our lives and limits conscious decision-making.

- Negative Anticipation: When we constantly worry about what could go wrong, this prevents us from enjoying the present, and having confidence in the future and causes anxiety.

- Social comparison: When we constantly compare ourselves and feel inadequate based on external standards.

- Perfectionism: When we demand ourselves to be perfect in all areas of life, this creates extreme self-demand and constant dissatisfaction.
- Disqualification of the positive: When we dismiss praise and achievements, thinking that we do not deserve them.
- Minimization of racial identity: When we dismiss the importance of our racial identity or deny its influence on personal experiences.
- Unfair social expectations: When we feel pressured to meet unrealistic social expectations of appearance, behavior and success.
- External invalidation: When we dismiss our own experiences of racial or gender discrimination due to lack of validation by others.
- Difficulty asking for help: When we feel that asking for emotional support or seeking help is a sign of weakness or vulnerability.

These distortions are thought patterns that many of us experience at some point in our lives. Recognizing them is the first step in challenging them and taking action to achieve a healthier, more realistic mindset.

Each of us is different, so these distortions can vary in their impact and frequency. Self-reflection and emotional self-care are powerful tools that can help us address them and foster emotional empowerment.

We must not allow these distortions to define our self-image or limit our potential.

Strategies for healthy thinking

Once we have identified the common distortions in our thinking, it is time to learn and apply strategies to have healthier and more realistic thoughts.

The way we think and perceive the world has a profound impact on our emotions and actions. By strengthening healthy thinking, we can grow emotionally and take control of our lives.

Some strategies that can help us are:

1. Daily Self-Affirmation: Every day, take a moment to affirm your qualities and abilities. Say out

loud or write positive affirmations about yourself. Acknowledge your worth and ability. For example, you can say to yourself, "I am strong, intelligent, and deserving of success in all areas of my life."

2. Questioning Negative Thoughts: When you find yourself thinking negatively, stop and ask yourself if those ideas are really true and based on evidence. Often, you will discover that they are distorted thoughts. For example, if you think, "I'm never good enough," ask yourself: What evidence do I have for that? What are the real facts?

3. Mindfulness Practice: Mindfulness involves being present in the present moment and observing your thoughts without judgment. This allows you to distance yourself from your negative thoughts and reduce their power over you. You can start with simple mindful breathing exercises or meditation.

4. Daily Gratitude: Take time every day to reflect on the things you are grateful for. Recognizing the

blessings in your life can shift your focus from the negative to the positive.

5. Emotional Self-Care: Practice essential self-care. Take care of yourself physically and emotionally. This includes getting enough rest, exercising, eating healthy, and seeking support when you need it. Take care of yourself as you deserve.

6. Positive Visualization: Visualize your goals and dreams as if they have already been accomplished. Imagine success and how it would feel to achieve it. Positive visualization can help you maintain an optimistic attitude and focus on your goals.

7. Open Communication: Talk about your thoughts and feelings with people you trust. Sometimes, just sharing how you feel can ease the emotional burden and give you a different perspective.

- Test the evidence: Question your thoughts and look for real evidence to back them up.
- Practice gratitude: Keep a gratitude journal and write down positive things in your life.

- Challenge catastrophic thinking: What is the worst that can happen? Is it as catastrophic as you imagine?
- Find the nuance: Avoid polarization and look for nuances in situations.
- Talk to yourself with kindness: Avoid negative labeling, practice self-acceptance and self-compassion.
- Practice mindfulness: Learn to live in the present and observe your thoughts without judging them.

These strategies will help you change your relationship with your thoughts, empower you and lead a more fulfilling life.

Chapter 6.

Listening to your Feelings

Want to know a powerful act of self-love and empowerment: Listen to your feelings. Knowing how to interpret your emotions and make decisions based on your feelings is a vital skill for your well-being and personal growth.

As Black women, our experiences are characterized by resilience, strength and deep emotional richness. But often, in the midst of the daily struggles and expectations we face, our emotions can be overlooked or even repressed.

Imagine that your emotions are like a language, a signaling system that guides you through life. Each emotion has an important message to convey to you. For example, joy may signal what fills you with satisfaction and brings joy to your life, while sadness may reveal what needs to be addressed or healed. Anger may indicate that your personal boundaries have been crossed, while gratitude may remind you of the blessings you have received.

But here's a trick: to hear that emotional language, you must first be willing to sit with yourself and pay attention. I can't say it's an easy process, as life can be noisy and often pushes us to move on without taking the time to process what we're feeling. But it is important that you take that time to reflect on your emotions; this is a great act of love for yourself.

When you take the time to interpret your emotions, you are also setting yourself up to make decisions that are more aligned with what you really need and want. Do you ever feel like you are living a life that doesn't belong to you? This could be because you've been making decisions based on what others expect of you or what you think you should do rather than what you feel deep in your heart.

When you trust your emotional guidance, you can make more authentic decisions. You can say Yes! to opportunities that fill you with joy and No! to those that drain you, so you can also set healthy boundaries, communicate your needs effectively, and seek relationships and friendships that nourish your soul instead of draining your energy.

How can you listen to your feelings? Here are some of the options we have:

- Emotion Journal: Write down your emotions in a journal. Describe what you are feeling and any events or thoughts related to that emotion. Over time, this will help you identify emotional patterns and better understand your reactions.
- Emotional Pause: When you feel an intense emotion, take a moment and take a deep breath, analyze what message that emotion is transmitting to you. What do you need at this moment? Is it an action you need to take?
- Emotional Wish List: Make a list of the emotions you most want to have in your life, as well as the activities or practices that would help you achieve

them. Then, you can gradually integrate them into your routine.

- Emotional Circle of Support: Find or create a circle of support, preferably of black women, with whom you can talk openly and honestly about your emotions and experiences. Sharing and receiving support can strengthen your emotional connection.

- Visualization: Close your eyes and visualize how you would feel if you lived a life aligned with your emotions and desires. Use this visualization as a source of inspiration and motivation.

As you begin to identify what you feel and interpret your emotions, you can begin to make decisions based on your feelings and what you really want to do, and you will discover a new strength and authenticity in your life.

You are the master of your own emotional destiny, and your ability to navigate it lies within you.

Trust yourself and your emotions, and you will see how your life will be filled with new vitality and meaning.

You have the power to be who you really are and live an authentic and fulfilling life!

Exercises and questions for reflection

Below, I suggest you do the following five exercises, all of which are designed to help you identify, understand and address your emotional needs:

<u>Exercise 1</u>

Letter to your inner child

Write a letter to your inner child. Speak with love and understanding. Ask her how she feels, what she needs and how you can best care for her.

1. What emotions came up as you were writing the letter?

____

____

____

____

____

2. What emotional needs do you identify in your inner child?

____

____

____

____

____

3. How do you feel about your inner child after writing the letter?

____

____

____

____

____

4. What concrete steps do you think you could take to meet the emotional needs of your inner child?

____

____

____

____

____

5. How do you think this will impact your current emotional well-being?

____

____

____

____

____

Exercise 2

Map of emotional needs

Draw a map that represents your emotional needs.

Identify the areas where you feel your needs are being met.

Then, identify those that may need more attention.

1. What areas of your life have your emotional needs most met?

____

____

____

____

____

2. In what areas do you feel your emotional needs are not being met?

____

____

____

____

____

3. How do you feel about recognizing these areas?

____

____

____

____

____

4. What steps can you take to begin to address those unmet emotional needs?

____

____

____

____

____

5. How do you think this will affect your overall well-being?

____

____

____

____

____

Exercise 3

Your emotional support tribe

Make a list of the people who are part of your emotional support tribe. Who are there to listen to you, support you and understand your emotions?

1. How does it make you feel to know that you have trusted people in your life?

   ____

   ____

   ____

   ____

   ____

2. How do you feel when you share your emotions with them?

   ____

   ____

   ____

   ____

   ____

3. What roles do these people play in your emotional life?

   ____

   ____

   ____

---

4. Is there anyone else you would like to include in your emotional support tribe?

5. How can you strengthen your relationships with these people and nurture your support network?

<u>Exercise 4</u>

Visualization of the satisfaction of needs

Close your eyes and visualize how you would feel if your deepest emotional needs were fully met. Imagine a life in which you feel loved, supported and understood.

1. What emotions did you experience in the visualization?

____

2. What emotional needs did you feel were met?

____

3. Is this visualization reflected in your life today?

____

____

____

____

____

4. What steps can you take to move closer to this vision?

____

____

____

____

____

5. What is your next concrete step in meeting your deep emotional needs?

____

____

____

____

____

<u>Exercise 5</u>

Emotional self-care ritual

Design an emotional self-care ritual that allows you to meet your emotional needs. It can be a relaxing bath, meditation, journaling, or any activity that connects you to yourself.

1. Which emotional self-care ritual did you choose?

____

____

____

____

____

2. How did you feel during and after the performance?

____

____

____

____

3. How do you plan to integrate this ritual into your daily or weekly routine?

____

____

____

____

____

4. How do you think this ritual will affect your emotional well-being in the long run?

____

____

____

____

____

5. What other emotional self-care rituals would you like to explore in the future?

____

____

____

6.1. Interpreting your emotions

Let's talk about something we all experience but sometimes struggle to fully understand: our emotions. Our experiences and feelings are unique, and it is important that we analyze the depth of what we feel. Let's discover together how we can interpret our emotions in a way that empowers us and makes us feel more connected to ourselves.

Instead of fearing your emotions or trying to ignore them, try to listen to what they are trying to tell you.

For example, sadness might be saying, "I need care and love," while joy might be saying, "This moment is precious; enjoy it to the fullest."

It is essential that we identify and name our emotions. Often, we feel a whirlwind of feelings and do not know exactly what is going on inside us; in these cases, ask yourself: "How do I feel at this moment?

Sometimes, our emotions can be intertwined, and that's okay. The important thing is to recognize them.

There are no "good" or "bad" emotions. All are valid and deserve to be felt and understood. Sadness, anger, fear and joy are all natural parts of being human.

Don't judge yourself for what you feel; on the contrary, look at it as an opportunity to get to know yourself better.

Your emotions are like a beacon guiding you in the dark, helping you understand what is important to you and what you need at any given moment. For example, if you feel anxiety before a difficult conversation, it could be a sign that you value honest communication. Learn to listen to these signals and act accordingly.

Questions for reflection

- How are you feeling right now? Try to name your emotions as specifically as possible.

- Have you noticed emotional patterns in your life? What emotions are most frequent?

- Can you identify any emotion that you have been preventing or repressing? Why do you think you do it?

- Think of a recent situation in which you experienced an intense emotion. What do you think that emotion was trying to tell you?

- How could you begin to use your emotions as guides in your daily life? Are there any actions you should take in response to your emotions?

6.2. Decisions based on feelings

Our emotions and how they influence our decisions are a powerful force that we sometimes underestimate. Our intuition and our feelings can be powerful guides to making decisions that truly resonate with who we are and what we value.

At this time, I want to encourage you to trust your ability to make decisions based on your feelings.

When we face important decisions, such as job changes, relationships or personal challenges, we can sometimes feel overwhelmed by the choices. It is in those moments when our emotions can be our best allies; when you are going through these circumstances, ask yourself, "How do I feel about this decision?"

Intuition is that inner voice that often manifests itself as a deep feeling in the gut or a sense of certainty. Learn to listen to and trust your intuition.

When faced with a crossroads, take a moment to close your eyes, take a deep breath and tune into that inner voice. Intuition can provide invaluable guidance.

While it is important to make decisions based on our feelings, it is also crucial to balance this with logical and reflective thinking. Take the time to evaluate the pros and cons of a decision and consider how it aligns with your personal values and long-term goals.

No decision is risk-free, and you may make mistakes along the way. But remember, every mistake is a learning opportunity. Don't beat yourself up for making decisions that didn't work out the way you expected; instead, use those experiences to grow and evolve.

Questions for reflection

Think of an important decision you have made in the past.

- Was it primarily based on logic or on your feelings?
- How did you feel after making that decision?
- Was it a choice that made you feel more authentic to yourself?
- When was the last time you trusted your intuition to make a decision? How did it turn out?

- Are there current decisions that will confront you? How do you feel about them?
- What steps can you take to balance your emotions with logical thinking when making important decisions?

Remember that your emotions are a valuable part of who you are and can guide you toward a life that resonates with your authenticity.

Don't be afraid to trust your feelings and your intuition. You are strong, wise and capable of making decisions that will lead you to your best self.

Chapter 7.

Addressing Deep Needs

A vital aspect of emotional empowerment is addressing our deep needs. As Black women, our emotional needs can be as different as our challenges. Understanding and meeting these needs are essential to our well-being and growth.

As we have seen above, sometimes our emotions can act as signals that something is not balanced enough in our lives, so it is very important to take the time to identify and understand what is behind our emotions. For example, anger may mask a need for justice or respect, while sadness may be related to a loss.

Once we identify our emotional needs, the next step is to meet them in a healthy way; however, this may involve setting clear boundaries in our relationships, seeking support from our community or even seeking professional counseling if necessary.

As Black women, we often find ourselves taking care of our families, friends and communities, but we must also remember that we deserve to take care of ourselves. Self-care is not synonymous with being selfish; on the contrary, it is an investment in our own well-being, which in turn allows us to be better caregivers for others.

Emotional empowerment is not a destination where we arrive and it's all over; rather, it is an ongoing journey. As we discover our emotions, identify our needs and learn to meet them, we become increasingly empowered and grow as individuals. This process allows us to face challenges with more resilience and live a more authentic and meaningful life.

Questions for reflection:

- What are some of the emotions you have experienced recently that might be related to underlying unmet needs?
- Have you identified an emotional need that you have been ignoring or putting off?

- What steps can you take to satisfy an underlying emotional need in your life?
- How can you balance your self-care with your responsibilities to others?
- What is your vision of an empowered and emotionally healthy life?

Recognizing and addressing our emotional needs is an act of self-love that not only strengthens us as women but also strengthens our communities.

Exercises and questions for reflection

<u>Exercise 1</u>

Identifying your needs

Think of a recent situation in which you experienced a strong emotion, positive or negative.

Reflect on what need might be related to that emotion.

Write down your thoughts and reflections.

1. What emotion did you experience in that situation?

____

____

____

____

____

2. Can you identify a need that might be related to that emotion?

____

____

____

____

____

3. How could you satisfy that need in a healthy way?

____

____

____

____

____

4. How did you feel as you reflected on this need related to your emotions?

____

____

____

____

____

5. What are some concrete steps you could take to meet that need in a healthy way?

____

____

____

____

____

<u>Exercise 2</u>

Prioritizing your needs

Make a list of the most important emotional needs you have at this very moment.

Then, rank all these emotional needs in order of priority.

1. What do you consider to be the emotional needs you need to address first? Why?

____

____

____

____

____

2. Identify which of your emotional needs are the most important at this time in your life.

____

____

____

____

____

3. What do you consider your most urgent emotional needs to be satisfied? Comment on the reason for your answer.

____

____

____

____

____

4. How do you feel about prioritizing your needs in this way?

____

____

____

____

____

5. Do you think some of your emotional needs are more difficult to prioritize than others? Explain the reason for your answer.

____

____

____

____

____

Exercise 3

Creating an action plan

Select one of your priority emotional needs identified in the previous exercise.

Then, develop a detailed action plan on how you can meet that need.

Include the concrete steps and deadlines you consider necessary.

1. Of all of them, which emotional need did you select and why?

____

____

____

____

____

2. What are the specific steps you can take to meet that need?

____

____

____

____

____

3. What is your first step and when will you take it?

____

____

____

____

____

4. How do you feel about having an action plan to meet your selected emotional need?

____

____

____

____

____

5. What obstacles do you anticipate in implementing this plan and how do you plan to overcome them?

____

____

____

____

____

Exercise 4

Sharing with your community

Think about how you can share your experiences and knowledge about emotional self-care with other black women in your community.

1. What advice would you offer them?

____

____

____

____

____

2. How do you think your experience in emotional self-care can benefit other black women?

____

____

____

____

____

3. What specific recommendations or resources would you share with them?

____

____

____

____

____

4. What is the first step you can take to start this conversation in your community?

____

____

____

____

____

5. What specific issues do you think will be most relevant to other black women in your community?

____

____

____

____

____

Exercise 5

Celebrating your achievements

Make a list of the accomplishments you have achieved in your journey toward emotional self-care.

These achievements may be large or small, but they are all important.

Take a moment to celebrate your successes and reflect on how you have become stronger.

1. What achievements have you made in your quest for emotional self-care?

____

____

____

____

____

2. How do you feel looking back on your progress?

____

____

____

____

____

3. What motivates you to keep working on your wellness?

____

____

____

____

____

4. How have you strengthened yourself along this journey to emotional self-care?

____

____

____

____

____

5. How do you plan to maintain your motivation and continue to work on your emotional well-being in the future?

____

____

____

____

These exercises are designed to help you deepen the process of addressing your emotional needs.

Each step you take brings you closer to a life of empowerment and fulfillment. Remember that your emotional well-being is a priority and that you deserve to care for yourself with love and compassion.

7.1. Identifying your underlying needs

Throughout our lives, the challenges we face can affect our emotions in a variety of ways, and identifying our underlying needs is an important part of emotional self-care and empowerment.

Sometimes, our emotions can seem overwhelming, confusing or difficult to understand. You may wonder why you feel a certain way in specific situations. The key to addressing these emotions is to distinguish the needs that underlie them.

Here are some suggestions to help you in this process:

- Listen carefully: When you experience an intense emotion, take a moment and listen to what your inner self is telling you. What need might be behind this emotion? For example, if you feel anger after a challenging conversation, the underlying need could be respect or understanding.

- Reflect on patterns: Notice if there are recurring patterns in your emotions - do you feel the same way in similar situations? This could indicate a consistent underlying need that you need to address.

- Talk to yourself: Sometimes, talking to yourself out loud or keeping an emotional journal can help you explore your deepest feelings and needs. You can ask yourself questions like, "What do I need right now to feel better?" or "What do I want to accomplish in this situation?"

- Seek support: Sharing your thoughts and emotions with friends, family members or mental health professionals can be valuable. Sometimes, others can offer perspectives that will help you identify underlying needs you may not have considered.

- Learn from your experiences: As you practice identifying your needs, you will learn more about yourself and your emotional patterns. This self-awareness will strengthen and help you on your journey to emotional self-care.

Remember that there are no wrong answers in this process. Identifying your underlying needs is an act of self-love and a crucial step toward emotional empowerment.

As you deepen your understanding of yourself, you will be better equipped to address your emotions and live an authentic and fulfilling life.

7.2. Meeting your emotional needs

As mentioned earlier, once you have identified your emotional needs, the next step is to meet them. We often find ourselves in the position of caregivers, always paying attention to the needs of others, but we must not forget to take care of our own emotional needs.

Some of the ways to meet these needs are:

- Value your alone time: Often, our lives are filled with responsibilities to our families, friends and communities. But don't forget that you also need time for yourself. Find moments to disconnect from the outside world and connect with yourself. This can be as simple as enjoying a quiet bath or taking a walk in nature.
- Set healthy boundaries: Learn to say "no" when necessary. Setting clear boundaries allows you to protect your emotional energy and avoid burnout. Don't be afraid to put your needs first.
- Seek emotional support: Talking to trusted friends or seeking the help of a therapist can be liberating. You don't have to carry your emotions and worries by yourself. Sharing your feelings

with others can ease the burden and provide valuable perspective.

- Take care of your physical well-being: The body and mind are connected. Be sure to take care of your physical health through a balanced diet, regular exercise and sufficient rest. A healthy body can help you better manage your emotions.

- Explore your passions: Often, our passions and hobbies take a back seat to our responsibilities. Spend time doing what you love and makes you feel alive. This can be anything from dance and music to writing or gardening.

- Practice self-care: Develop a self-care routine that works for you. This could include meditation, yoga, mindfulness or any activity that helps you feel at peace with yourself.

- Celebrate your successes: No matter how small or large, celebrate your accomplishments and your moments of joy. Recognize your successes and remember that you deserve love and happiness.

- Seek out community: Connecting with other Black women who share your experiences can be comforting. Sharing stories and mutual support can be a source of empowerment and strength.

- Learn to forgive yourself: We all make mistakes and face challenges. Don't be too hard on yourself. Forgiveness, both toward yourself and others is a liberating act that allows you to move forward.

- Seek professional help if needed: If you feel your emotions are overwhelming or difficult to manage, don't hesitate to seek the help of a mental health professional. There is no shame in asking for support when you need it.

Taking care of yourself allows you to be the best version of yourself and be in a position to support those around you.

Chapter 8.

Lessons from the Zen Masters

Let's talk about the lessons of Zen masters, a source of ancient wisdom, which can be a guide on our path to self-care, emotional empowerment and inner peace, especially in the context and challenges we face as black women.

You may be wondering what Zen is; it is a branch of Buddhism which has its roots in the ancient spiritual tradition of Asia. It originates in India and is then transmitted to China and Japan.

Zen is characterized by its focus on meditation and mindfulness to achieve enlightenment and inner peace. Zen teachings emphasize the importance of direct experience and non-judgmental observation.

Now, the lessons of Zen masters are pearls of wisdom that have been passed down through generations.

These teachings focus on self-reflection, mindfulness and a deep understanding of the nature of the mind. That is, rather than providing definitive answers, Zen challenges us to question and explore our own perceptions and beliefs.

The lessons of Zen masters have a clear purpose and that is to help us find mental clarity, serenity and understanding amidst the chaos and emotional storms of life. They provide us with tools for connection with ourselves and the world around us.

There are many benefits of Zen Lessons; some of them are:

- Inner peace: Zen lessons teach us to calm the mind and live in the present. This allows us to release stress and anxiety, finding peace that comes from acceptance and understanding.
- Resilience: By learning to observe our emotions and thoughts without judgment, we strengthen our resilience. We become more capable of facing challenges with grace and determination.

- Mental clarity: Zen helps us see through our thoughts and concerns, allowing us to make decisions that are more conscious and aligned with our values.

- Interpersonal connection: Zen teachings encourage us to recognize the humanity in everyone, fostering empathy and more authentic communication in our relationships.

- Alignment with purpose: Helps us discover our path in life and find deeper meaning. They guide us towards a life of authenticity and meaning.

To apply these lessons in your life, consider incorporating meditation and mindfulness into your daily routine. Spend time in quiet reflection, pay attention to your breathing and practice non-judgmental observation of your thoughts and emotions. This will help you cultivate inner peace and connection to the essence of your being.

In a world that can often be chaotic and challenging, especially for us, the lessons of Zen masters can be an enlightening guide. They remind us that peace and strength reside within ourselves and that we can find calm in the midst of the storm. They are a reminder that we are capable of empowering ourselves and transforming our lives through inner wisdom.

Zen invites us to explore our inner world and embrace the beauty and strength found in our souls.

I hope these lessons guide you on your journey to authenticity and empowerment.

Exercises and questions for reflection

Exercise 1

Mindfulness Meditation

Perform a mindfulness meditation for 10 minutes.

Find a quiet place, sit comfortably and focus your attention on your breathing.

Observe your thoughts without judgment and refocus on your breath whenever your mind wanders.

1. What thoughts or emotions came up during your meditation?

____

____

____

____

____

2. How do you feel after meditation?

____

____

____

____

____

3. Do you notice any difference in your level of calmness or mental clarity?

____

____

____

____

4. How could you integrate mindfulness into your daily life?

____

____

____

____

____

5. What obstacles did you face in practicing mindfulness and how can you overcome them?

____

____

____

____

____

<u>Exercise 2</u>

Gratitude Journal

Start a gratitude journal where each day you write down three things you are grateful for, from a sunrise to a meaningful conversation.

1. What impact did keeping a gratitude journal have on your state of mind?

____

____

____

____

____

2. What did you discover about the things you are grateful for?

____

____

____

____

3. How did this exercise help you appreciate the present more?

____

____

____

____

____

4. Was there a day when it was difficult for you to find things to be thankful for? If so, how did you deal with it?

____

____

____

____

____

5. How can you maintain this habit over the long term?

____

____

____

____

____

<u>Exercise 3</u>

Conscious Walking

Take a mindful walk in a natural setting or even in your neighborhood.

Walk slowly and pay attention to every step you take; feel the sensation of the ground under your feet.

Also, pay attention to the sounds you hear around you and the smells you perceive during the walk.

1. How did it feel to pay conscious attention to your surroundings while walking?

____

____

____

____

____

2. What details did you notice that you would normally overlook?

3. How do you connect with nature or your urban environment differently?

4. What lessons or insights did you gain?

5. How can you incorporate mindful walking into your regular routine?

____

____

____

____

____

<u>Exercise 4</u>

Deep Breathing Practice

Spend 5 minutes every day practicing deep breathing.

Sit in a quiet place, inhale deeply for 4 seconds, hold your breath for 4 seconds and exhale for 4 seconds.

Repeat this process several times, as many times as you consider necessary.

1. How do you feel after the deep breathing practice?

____

____

____

____

____

2. Do you notice any difference in your stress or anxiety level?

____

____

____

____

____

3. How can you use this technique in moments of tension or stress that come up during the day?

____

____

____

____

____

4. In what areas of your life do you think deep breathing can be most beneficial? Detail the reason for your answer.

____

____

____

____

____

5. How can you remind yourself to practice deep breathing regularly? Would you consider doing it always at the same time?

____

____

____

____

____

Exercise 5

Empathic Communication

Choose an important conversation in your life and practice empathetic communication.

Listen preemptively to the other person, show understanding and avoid judging or interrupting.

Make a conscious attempt to understand their emotions and needs.

1. How did the other person feel about being heard in this way?

____

____

____

____

____

2. What did you discover about your emotions and needs?

____

____

____

____

____

3. How do you feel about communicating empathetically?

____

____

____

____

____

4. In what future situations could you apply this active listening skill?

____

____

____

____

____

5. What did you learn about the importance of empathy in communication?

____

____

____

____

____

8.1. Applying Zen wisdom to your life

Let's talk about how we can apply Zen wisdom to our lives as Black women. The Zen tradition offers us valuable teachings that can help us move forward confident in the face of challenges and enjoy the joys we encounter along the way.

Let's look at how we can incorporate these lessons in our quest for empowerment and inner peace.

- Mindfulness in Everyday Life

Zen teaches us to pay full attention to each moment. This means being present in our daily activities, whether it is cooking, walking or simply breathing. We often face a wide variety of responsibilities and expectations. Practicing mindfulness will allow us to approach our tasks and challenges with calm and clarity.

- The Importance of Breathing

Conscious breathing is a fundamental part of Zen practice. It helps us find inner peace and cope with stress. As we face challenges such as racism and discrimination, deep breathing can be a powerful tool for maintaining our calm and resilience.

- Acceptance and Non-judgment

Zen teaches us to accept things as they are, without judgment. As black women, we often face external judgments and stereotypes, practicing acceptance and non-judgment allows us to free ourselves from the burden of others' expectations and find self-acceptance.

- Empathic Communication

Zen invites us to listen and understand others with empathy. In a world where our voices are often minimized, empathetic communication allows us to build meaningful connections and foster positive change.

- Peace in the midst of chaos

Zen practice shows us that inner peace is possible even in the midst of chaos. As we strive for justice and equality, let us remember that our inner strength and peace are our most powerful allies.

- The Power of Gratitude

Zen teaches us to appreciate each moment and to be grateful for what we have. Practicing gratitude helps us maintain a positive outlook, even when we face obstacles.

- Living in the Present

Zen reminds us that the past no longer exists and the future is uncertain. The only reality is the present. As black women, we can find power and freedom by living fully in the now.

- Resilience as a Strength

Zen tradition shows us that resilience is a form of strength. As black women, we are inherently resilient. We can face challenges and overcome them with grace.

- Community and Mutual Support

Zen teaches us the importance of community. Let us seek mutual support and solidarity among black women. Together, we are stronger.

- Celebrating Our Identity

Ultimately, Zen reminds us of the importance of celebrating who we are. Our identity as Black women is valuable and unique. Let's face the world with pride and authenticity.

8.2. Peace in the midst of chaos

Let me talk about finding peace in the midst of chaos. Our lives are often filled with challenges and tumultuous moments, but we are also incredibly resilient and able to find calm in even the most difficult circumstances.

- The Chaos Surrounding Us

We know that the world can be a chaotic place. We struggle with racism, discrimination and injustice. At times, it seems that chaos surrounds us on all sides. But remember that inside you is a place of peace that no one can take away.

- The Power of Self-contemplation

Self-contemplation is a powerful tool. When you feel overwhelmed by chaos, take a moment to look inward. Reflect on your emotions and needs. Connect with yourself and find that inner calm.

- The Importance of Breathing

Conscious breathing is like an anchor in the middle of a storm. When everything around you feels agitated, your breath can be a source of stability. Take a moment to breathe deeply and find balance.

- Embracing Impermanence

Zen teaches us that everything in life is impermanent. Moments of chaos will not last forever. Learn to embrace impermanence and remember that even in the darkest moments, the light will eventually return.

- The Importance of Community

In times of chaos, remember that you are not alone. Our community of Black women is an endless source of support and strength. Reach out to your sisters and share your burdens. Together, we are stronger.

- Resilience as a Virtue

Our resilience is a virtue. We have faced adversity throughout history and emerged stronger. Trust in your ability to overcome any challenge that comes your way.

- Authenticity in Adversity

Maintain your authenticity in the midst of chaos. Don't let yourself be changed by circumstances. You are valuable and authentic in any situation.

- The Search for Inner Peace

Inner peace is a gift you can give yourself. Find moments of tranquility and connection with yourself. Find ways to nurture your emotional well-being.

- The Power of Hope

Hope is a bright light in the darkness. Keep hope alive for a more just and equitable world. Our struggle is a testament to that hope.

- Celebrating Our Resistance

Finally, celebrate your resilience. Every day you face the chaos and move forward is a victory. You are a guerrilla, and the world needs your strength.

In the midst of chaos, remember that you carry peace within you. You are strong and courageous. Let us continue to support each other, finding calm in the midst of the storm and working together for a better future.

Conclusion of Volume I

We have reached the end of Volume I of our journey towards emotional self-care, empowerment and inner strength. Throughout these eight chapters, we have discovered the complex nature of emotions, demystifying them and understanding how they influence our lives. We have learned to connect with our feelings, discovering unique emotional experiences that shape our identity.

We have delved into the origin of our emotional responses, identifying triggers and learning how to manage our emotions effectively. We have also explored the link between body and mind, understanding how to balance our emotions to promote holistic wellness.

During the reading, we have learned to challenge common thinking distortions, use strategies to maintain healthy thoughts, learn to listen to our emotions, interpret them and make decisions based on our feelings.

In addition, we have understood the importance of identifying our underlying emotional needs and the importance of satisfying them to nurture our well-being, and we have applied Zen wisdom to our lives, finding peace in the midst of chaos.

But this journey is not over yet. Volume II awaits us with more tools and tips to strengthen our emotional resilience, maintain inner calm, release constructive emotions and live authentically.

I invite you to continue this journey, where you will find even more exercises, tips and guidance to continue strengthening your inner strength.

Thank you for joining me. Together, we are a powerful community that supports each other in the pursuit of an emotionally healthy and empowered life.

Let's keep moving forward!

VOLUME II

Emotional Well-Being

Introduction to Volume II

We have traveled a meaningful journey through Volume I of this book, discovered the complexities of our emotions and learning to understand them, demystified our feelings, explored how they affect our lives and begun to discover the power of self-reflection. Now, we are ready to take the next step toward our continued emotional self-care and empowerment.

In this Volume II, we will delve even deeper into the world of emotional well-being. We will address fundamental topics that will help you stay calm in the midst of chaos, release emotions constructively, cultivate resilience, rediscover joy and live authentically.

We will also learn how to find inner peace and how to maintain it in your daily life. In addition, I will provide you with practical tools to prioritize your well-being and establish a life of sustained self-care.

This book is not only about understanding your emotions; it is about learning to navigate them and use them as resources to live a full and authentic life.

Each chapter is designed to give you practical tips and proven strategies that will help you embrace your inner power and take care of yourself in a sustainable way.

Don't forget that the process of self-care and emotional empowerment is an ongoing journey, and each step you take brings you closer to the strongest and most authentic version of yourself.

At the end of this volume, you will find additional self-care exercises, tips on how to find and create a supportive community, and a guide to creating your own personalized self-care plan.

You are about to enter a world of self-discovery, growth and emotional well-being. Your emotional well-being is a priority, and you deserve to care for yourself with love and compassion.

Continue with enthusiasm and confidence because your journey to emotional empowerment has no limits.

Chapter 1.

Maintaining Inner Calm

One valuable quality that can make a difference in our lives is inner calm. In the midst of the busy world we live in and the chaos of everyday life, the ability to remain calm is a source of strength and resilience, especially for us who often face additional challenges and pressures.

Inner calm is not just the absence of stress or conflict; it is the ability to maintain serenity even when emotional storms surround us. Here are some strategies that can help you cultivate that inner calm:

- Mindfulness: Practicing mindfulness allows you to be present in the moment, observing your thoughts and emotions without judgment. This can help reduce emotional reactivity and respond to situations in a more balanced way.
- The search for inner peace: Spend time in activities that bring you peace and joy, such as

meditation, reading, music, art or just being in nature. These activities nourish your soul and help you recharge your energy.

- Set healthy boundaries: Learn to say "no" when necessary and set clear limits on both your relationships and responsibilities. This will help you avoid overload and burnout.

- Mindful breathing is a powerful tool for staying calm. When you feel overwhelmed or anxious, take a moment to breathe deeply. This simple practice can help you reduce stress and regain mental clarity.

For us, life often involves facing turbulent situations. We may face racial discrimination, cultural expectations and social pressures. However, our ability to maintain inner calm can be our greatest strength.

No matter how difficult the circumstances, we always have the ability to find a moment of calm, a deep breath, and remind ourselves that we deserve peace of mind.

Keep in the back of your mind that you are not alone. Share these strategies with other black women who may need them and offer them your support. Together, we can uplift and strengthen each other in the search for inner calm.

Remember that your emotional well-being is a priority and that you deserve to live with serenity in the midst of chaos.

Here are five exercises related to the theme of maintaining inner calm, along with five questions for each.

These exercises are designed to help you deepen your understanding and practice of inner calm.

Exercises and questions for reflection

<u>Exercise 1</u>

Conscious Breathing

Perform a short session of conscious breathing. Find a quiet place, sit comfortably and close your eyes.

Then, take ten mindful breaths, paying attention to each inhalation and exhalation. Afterwards, reflect on your experience.

1. How do you feel before starting the conscious breathing session?

   ____

   ____

   ____

   ____

   ____

2. Do you notice any changes in your emotional or mental state after completing the ten breaths?

   ____

   ____

   ____

   ____

   ____

3. What obstacles, if any, did you encounter in trying to focus on your breathing?

____

____

____

____

____

4. How can you incorporate mindful breathing into your daily routine to maintain inner calm?

____

____

____

____

____

5. What did you learn from this practice that you can apply in stressful situations?

____

____

____

____

____

<u>Exercise 2</u>

Mindfulness in Daily Routine

Choose a daily activity, such as washing dishes or walking

Practice mindfulness while doing it.

Focus on every detail and sensation associated with that activity.

Then, reflect on your experience.

Then answer the following five questions:

1. What daily activity did you choose to practice mindfulness?

   ____

   ____

   ____

   ____

   ____

2. Did you notice differences between mindfulness activity in comparison and automatically?

____

____

____

____

____

3. Was it difficult, were you distracted by practicing mindfulness?

____

____

____

____

____

4. How can you integrate mindfulness into more aspects of your daily life?

____

____

____

____

____

5. What benefits do you experience from practicing mindfulness in an everyday activity?

____

____

____

____

____

Exercise 3

Setting Healthy Boundaries

Identify a situation or relationship where you need to set healthier boundaries and consider how you might communicate those boundaries effectively.

1. What situation or relationship did you identify where you need to set healthier boundaries?

____

____

____

____

____

2. Why do you set these limits?

____

____

____

____

____

3. How do you feel about communicating your boundaries in this situation?

____

____

____

____

____

4. What strategies or keywords could you use to communicate your boundaries effectively?

____

____

____

____

____

5. What steps can you take to implement these healthy boundaries?

____

____

____

____

____

Exercise 4

Self-Care Practice

Create a list of self-care activities that will help you maintain inner calm. Please select one of those activities and do it during this week. Reflect.

1. What self-care activities did you include in your list?

____

____

____

____

____

2. Why, out of all the activities on the list, did you choose that particular activity to do this week?

____

____

____

____

____

3. How did you feel before, during and after performing the self-care activity?

____

____

____

____

____

4. What obstacles, if any, did you encounter in making time for self-care?

____

____

____

____

____

5. How can you more regularly incorporate these self-care practices into your life?

____

____

____

____

____

Exercise 5

Sharing with the Community

Share a strategy or experience to maintain inner calm, what was it like and what did you learn?

1. What strategy or experience do you choose to share with someone in your community?

____

____

____

____

____

2. Share the information with another black woman. How did it feel?

____

____

____

____

____

3. Were there any challenges in communicating this strategy or experience?

____

____

____

____

____

4. What questions or comments were raised?

____

____

____

____

____

5. What did you learn from this sharing experience and how can you apply it in the future?

____

____

____

____

____

1.1. Calming strategies

I know that life can be a whirlwind of emotions and challenges, and at times, it can feel overwhelming. But I want to remind you that you have within you the power to find calm in the midst of any storm. Here are some strategies that have been helpful to many of us:

- Mindful breathing: Sometimes, all you need to do is stop for a moment and take a deep breath. Mindful breathing can help reduce stress and anxiety. Close your eyes, inhale deeply through your nose for a count of four, then exhale slowly through your mouth. Repeat this process several times until you feel calmness begin to return.

- Mediation and mindfulness: Meditation and mindfulness are powerful tools for finding inner calm. Take a few minutes each day to meditate and practice mindfulness. This will help you to be present in the moment and stop worrying about the past or the future.

- Time for yourself: Don't underestimate the importance of taking care of yourself. Find time in your routine to do what makes you happy. Whether it's reading a book, taking a walk in nature or just relaxing, it's essential to set aside time for yourself.

- Talk to someone you trust: Sometimes, sharing your feelings with someone you trust can ease a heavy emotional burden. Find a friend, family member or mental health professional with whom you can talk openly.

- Exercise: Physical activity is a great way to release tension and promote calm. Find a form of exercise that you enjoy, whether it's dancing, walking, yoga or any other activity that makes you feel good.

- Set healthy boundaries: Don't be afraid to say "no" when necessary and set boundaries to protect your emotional well-being. Remember that taking care of yourself is a priority.

- Connecting with the community: Sharing with other Black women who understand your experiences can be a source of support and calm. Seek out online or in-person groups or communities where you can connect with people who share your experiences.

- Find time for laughter: Laughter is a powerful remedy for stress. Take time to enjoy joyful moments with friends or family. Don't underestimate the value of a good laugh.

Remember that inner calm is a skill you can cultivate with practice and patience. No matter how challenging life may be at times, you have the strength to face any adversity.

These strategies can be your guide on the road to serenity.

1.2. Breathe and relax.

Throughout life, we face a number of challenges and responsibilities that can lead us to feel overwhelmed and tense. At those times, I want to remind you of the importance of taking a breath and relaxing.

Here are some tips that can help you find that space of tranquility:

- Find your quiet space: Find a place in your home or in nature where you feel comfortable and at peace. It can be a corner with soft cushions or your favorite garden. This will be your haven for relaxation.
- Conscious breathing: Breathing is a powerful tool for finding calm. Sit comfortably and close your

eyes. Inhale deeply through your nose, feeling the air fill your lungs. Then, exhale slowly through your mouth. Repeat this process several times, concentrating on each inhalation and exhalation.

- Visualization: Imagine a place that makes you feel safe and relaxed. It can be a quiet beach, a serene forest or any other environment that inspires peace. Close your eyes and visualize every detail of that place: the sounds, the smells, the feel of the breeze. Let this visualization transport you to a state of relaxation.

- Yoga or stretching: Practicing yoga or a gentle stretching routine can help you release tension in your body. Follow a series of slow, mindful movements to relax muscles and improve circulation.

- Relaxing music: Listening to soft, soothing music can be an effective way to calm the mind. Create a playlist with your favorite songs that will help you unwind and relax.

- Relaxing bath: A warm bath with bath salts or essential oils can be a rejuvenating experience. Immerse yourself in the water and allow yourself to relax completely.

- Screen-free time: Set aside time each day to disconnect from electronic devices such as phones and computers. This screen-free time will allow you to be present in the moment and reduce stress.

- Massage or self-massage: A gentle massage or self-massage can help release tension built up in the body. Use oil or cream to massage your muscles and relax.

- Gratitude journal: Before bedtime, write down three things you are grateful for in your gratitude journal. This will help you focus on the positive things in your life and reduce stress.

- Ask for support: Don't hesitate to seek support from friends, family or mental health professionals if you feel the stress is overwhelming. Sharing your concerns and emotions can ease the burden.

You deserve moments of peace and relaxation in your life. No matter how busy your schedule is, taking care of your emotional well-being is essential. Take a deep breath and give yourself permission to relax.

You are strong and able to find the inner calm you need.

Chapter 2.

Emotional Liberation

Emotional liberation allows us to face, express and transform those intense emotions in a healthy and constructive way.

When we experience intense emotions, it is natural to seek an outlet. However, it is important to choose a form of venting that is beneficial to our mental and emotional health.

Here are some ways to perform constructive emotional venting:

- Write down your feelings: Keeping an emotional journal is a powerful tool. Write down what you are feeling without censorship. This helps you process your emotions and understand what is going on inside you.

- Talk to someone you trust: Sharing your emotions with a close friend or therapist can be liberating. Sometimes, expressing what we feel out loud allows us to see things from a different perspective and find solutions.

- Practicing creative activities: painting, drawing, dancing or playing music are wonderful ways to release emotions. Creativity allows you to express yourself without words and connect deeply with yourself.

Once you've released your emotions, it's time to give them a new purpose. Here's how you can transform that emotional energy into something positive:

- Physical exercise: Exercise is a powerful way to release endorphins, which are neurotransmitters that improve mood. Walking, running, swimming or practicing yoga are excellent choices.
- Meditation and mindfulness: These practices help you stay calm and focused on the present. They allow you to observe your thoughts and emotions without judgment.
- Volunteering: Helping others can be a rewarding way to channel your emotional energy.

Contributing to your community connects you to a greater purpose and gives you a sense of fulfillment.

- Learn and grow: Intense emotions can sometimes be a sign that something in your life needs to change. Use this energy to identify areas for improvement and take steps to grow and evolve.

Remember, emotions are a fundamental part of being human, and we should not fear them. Learning to release them in a constructive way and transforming that energy can lead us to a place of greater emotional balance and inner strength.

Exercises and questions for reflection

<u>Exercise 1</u>

Emotional release meditation

Have a meditation session for emotional release.

Find a quiet place, sit comfortably and focus your attention on the emotion you wish to release.

Visualize how that emotion slowly dissolves, leaving space for calm.

You can find guided meditations online to help you in this process.

1. What emotion do you choose for the emotional release meditation?

   ____

   ____

   ____

   ____

   ____

2. How did you feel during the meditation?

   ____

   ____

   ____

   ____

3. Do you notice any changes in your emotional state after meditation?

4. Did you find this exercise helpful in releasing emotion?

5. Would you consider including meditation regularly in your emotional self-care routine?

<u>Exercise 2</u>

Constructive internal dialogue

When facing an intense emotion, pay attention to your internal dialogue.

Try to replace your negative or self-critical thoughts with much more positive and compassionate affirmations.

Keep track of your thoughts and the change in your perspective.

1. What kind of internal dialogue do you experience when you face an intense emotion?

____

____

____

____

____

2. Were you able to identify negative or self-critical thoughts?

____

____

____

____

____

3. How did those thoughts make you feel?

____

____

____

____

____

4. What positive affirmations do you use to change your perspective?

____

____

____

____

____

5. What impact did this change have on your emotional well-being?

____

____

____

____

____

Exercise 3

Emotional liberation rituals

Create a personal emotional release ritual.

1. What emotional release ritual did you create?

____

____

____

____

____

2. What inspired you to choose this particular ritual?

____

____

____

____

____

3. How do you feel about performing this ritual?

____

____

____

____

____

4. Do you experience relief or emotional release?

____

____

____

____

____

5. Would you consider incorporating this ritual into your life on a regular basis?

____

____

____

____

____

Exercise 4

Transformation visualization

Please close your eyes, imagine a calm and safe place, visualize your emotions as objects, and observe how you transform them into something lighter and calmer.

1. What peaceful place did you visualize in your mind?

____

____

____

____

____

2. How do you represent your intense emotions in
that visualization?

____

____

____

____

____

3. What changes did you observe in these
emotional representations?

____

____

____

____

____

4. How did you feel during this visualization
exercise?

____

____

____

____

____

5. Do you think this transformation technique could be useful in moments of intense emotion?

____

____

____

____

____

Exercise 5

Creation of a space for emotional liberation

Dedicate a physical space in your home where you can release emotions in a safe and constructive way, including elements such as pillows, paper, colors, music or any object that helps you express your emotions.

1. How did you design your release space?

____

____

____

____

____

2. What elements did you include in that space?

____

____

____

____

____

3. What do you feel in your place to release emotions?

____

____

____

____

____

4. Have you used this space in moments of intense emotion?

____

____

____

____

____

5. What impact has it had on your emotional well-being?

____

____

____

____

____

These additional exercises are designed to provide you with additional tools for emotional release. Each can be a valuable addition to your emotional self-care toolbox.

Remember that you have the power to transform and release your emotions in a healthy and empowering way.

2.1. Constructive Emotional Relief

I know that life can test us in many ways, and at times, emotions can feel like an overwhelming burden; inside us, we carry unique stories and experiences that can sometimes trigger intense emotions. But I want to remind you that constructive emotional venting can be a powerful tool in our journey to wellness.

When we face intense emotions, it is critical to find healthy ways to release that emotional energy. Sometimes, society has told us that we should be strong and keep our emotions silent, but that is neither sustainable nor healthy. We need spaces and methods to express ourselves.

Here are some strategies for constructive emotional venting that might help you:

- Honest dialogue: Talking with close friends, family members or trusted therapists can be an effective way to release emotions. Don't be afraid to share your feelings with supportive people.
- Therapeutic writing: Keeping a journal or writing letters to yourself can be a powerful way to process your emotions. Sometimes, putting words to feelings can ease the emotional burden.
- Physical activity: Regular exercise, whether it's running, dancing, yoga or any activity you enjoy, can release endorphins and help you feel better emotionally.
- Art and creativity: Artistic expression, such as painting, drawing, singing or dancing, can be a beautiful way to release emotions. It doesn't matter if you are a professional artist or just want to try something new; the important thing is that you feel free to express yourself.
- Meditation and mindfulness: Meditation allows you to observe your thoughts and emotions

without judgment. This practice can help you gain clarity and inner calm.

- Community support: Seek out black women's groups or communities that allow you to share your experiences. Sometimes, just knowing that you are not alone in your emotions can be comforting.

Questions for reflection

- How do you feel as you consider the idea of releasing your emotions in a constructive way?
- Have you tried any of the emotional venting strategies mentioned above?
- Which of these strategies do you think might be most effective for you?
- How will you commit to incorporating constructive emotional venting into your daily life?
- What steps can you take today to begin practicing constructive emotional venting?

Dear sister, remember that our emotions are valid, and we deserve to take care of ourselves in a way that empowers us.

Constructive emotional venting is an act of self-love and self-respect.

2.2. Transforming emotional energy

Imagine that your emotions are like water in a river. When the river overflows, it can cause havoc and destruction. But if we learn to redirect and channel that water, we can use it to nourish fields and bring life to our environment. Similarly, our emotions can be transformed into a powerful force for positive change.

Here are some ways you can learn to transform your emotional energy:

- Creativity and expression: Channel your emotions in creative ways. You can write poetry, create art, compose music or express yourself in any way that makes you feel free and authentic.

- Activism and advocacy: Many black women have used their emotional energy to lead movements for social change. You can turn your passion into concrete actions to advocate for justice and equality.
- Self-care: Learn to care for yourself in a compassionate way. Self-care allows you to recharge your energy and maintain emotional balance.
- Mutual support: Share your emotions with other black women. Sometimes, talking to someone who understands your experiences can be a powerful way to release and transform emotional energy.
- Education and growth: Use your emotional energy to learn and grow. Education can be a powerful avenue for personal empowerment and creating positive change in your life and community.

Questions for reflection:

- How do you feel as you consider the idea of transforming your emotional energy into something positive?

- Have you experienced times when your emotions prompted you to take significant action?

- What forms of creative expression are you interested in or would you like to explore?

- How can you incorporate self-care practices into your daily routine to manage your emotional energy?

- What concrete steps can you take today to begin transforming your emotional energy in a way that is meaningful to you and your community?

Remember that your emotional energy is a source of power and potential. As you learn to transform it constructively, you can influence your life and the world around you in amazing ways.

Chapter 3.

Tools for Resilience

Let's talk about resilience. It's a powerful word that is often associated with the ability to overcome challenges and adversity with grace and strength.

Resilience is like a muscle that you can strengthen with time and practice. Here are some ways you can develop and nurture your resilience:

- Emotional self-awareness: Understanding and recognizing your own emotions is the first step in building resilience. Learning to listen to what your heart and mind are telling you will help you face challenges with a clearer perspective.

- Support Network: Connecting with other Black women who share your experiences can be an invaluable source of support. Our community is a haven where you can find encouragement, understanding and solidarity.

- Resilient Mindset: Cultivating a resilient mindset means adopting a "never give up" attitude. Recognizing that obstacles are opportunities for growth and learning can help maintain a positive attitude in the midst of challenges.

- Overcoming challenges with grace: Life is full of challenges, but no matter how difficult they are, you have the ability to overcome them with grace. Here are some strategies that can help you:

- Acceptance and adaptation: Accepting circumstances that you cannot change and adapting to them is a sign of strength. Life is fluid, and learning to flow with it will make you more resilient.

- Set goals and priorities: Setting clear goals and priorities gives you a sense of direction. Focusing on what really matters can help you stay focused and overcome obstacles.

- Continuous self-care: Self-care is an act of self-love. No matter how busy you are, don't neglect your physical and emotional well-being.
- Celebrate your victories: Recognize your accomplishments, even the small ones. Every small step forward is a reason for celebration and a reminder of your ability to overcome challenges.

Questions for reflection:

- How do you feel about your own resilience right now?
- What are some strategies you have used to overcome challenges in the past?
- What does resilience mean to you and how would you like to develop it further?
- Do you have a support network of other black women you can confide in and share your experiences?
- What is a current challenge you face and how can you apply resilience tools to address it gracefully?

Remember that you are stronger than you think. Your ability to develop resilience and overcome challenges is an intrinsic part of your being. On your journey to empowerment, resilience is a valuable tool that will help you face any storm with grace and determination.

Exercises and questions for reflection

Here are five exercises related to the topic of resilience:

<u>Exercise 1</u>

Emotional Self-Awareness

Reflect on a recent situation in which you experienced an intense emotion, either positive or negative. Then answer these questions:

1. What emotion did you experience in that situation?

____

____

____

____

____

2. How did you recognize and manage that emotion in the moment?

____

____

____

____

____

3. What personal thoughts and beliefs influenced your emotional reaction?

____

____

____

____

____

4. What could you do differently in a similar situation in the future to be more resilient?

____

____

____

____

____

5. How do you feel as you reflect on your ability to recognize your emotions and manage them appropriately?

____

____

____

____

____

<u>Exercise 2</u>

Support Community

Think about black women you have interacted with in your life or have knowledge of their lives.

Now, think of three of these women who are part of your support network or whom you admire for their resilience.

1. What resilience qualities or strategies do they have?

____

____

____

____

____

2. How have they inspired or supported you in difficult times?

____

____

____

____

____

3. Have you shared your own experiences of resilience with them? What has that experience been like?

____

____

____

____

____

4. How can they further strengthen their community of support?

____

____

____

____

____

5. How does it feel to know that you have a strong support network in your life?

____

____

____

____

<u>Exercise 3</u>

Acceptance and Adaptation

Think of a challenging situation you are facing. Then, answer these questions:

1. How do you feel about this challenge at the moment?

____

____

____

____

____

2. What aspects of the situation can you accept as they are?

____

____

____

____

____

3. How can you adapt to this situation effectively?

____

____

____

____

____

4. What is the first step you can take to approach this challenge with grace?

____

____

____

____

____

5. What motivates you to face this challenge with determination?

____

____

____

____

____

<u>Exercise 4</u>

Continuous Self-Care

Make a list of five self-care activities or practices that will help you stay resilient and in balance.

Please answer these questions below:

1. Which of these activities are you already incorporating into your life?

____

____

____

____

____

2. Which ones would you like to explore or adopt in your daily routine?

____

____

____

____

____

3. How do you feel when you make time for self-care?

____

____

____

____

____

4. Which self-care activity do you consider most important to your well-being?

____

____

____

____

____

5. How do you plan to integrate these self-care activities into your life on an ongoing basis?

____

____

____

____

____

<u>Exercise 5</u>

Celebrating your Victories

Make a list of 5 accomplishments or moments of overcoming challenges that you have experienced in your life.

1. Which of these achievements are particularly significant to you?

    ____

    ____

    ____

    ____

    ____

2. How do you feel about overcoming these challenges?

    ____

    ____

    ____

____

____

3. What did you learn from these experiences of overcoming?

____

____

____

____

____

4. How do you apply the strength and resilience you demonstrate in those moments to your challenges?

____

____

____

____

____

5. Which of these victories has taught you the importance of resilience and how do you apply it?

____

____

____

____

____

3.1. Developing your resilience

Let's talk about resilience, that strength we carry within us that allows us to overcome challenges, stay strong and shine even in the darkest moments.

I know that in our community of black women, we have faced unique obstacles throughout history, but we have also demonstrated incredible resilience.

Here, I want to share some ideas on how we can develop and strengthen our resilience together.

- Knowing your inner strength: Resilience starts from the inside. Take a moment to reflect on the times in your life when you have overcome challenges. What has kept you going? How did it feel to look back and see how strong you are?

Acknowledge that inner strength and hold it close during difficult times.

- Taking care of yourself: Self-care is a crucial part of resilience. Be sure to take care of your body and mind. This can include activities such as exercise, meditation, healthy eating and adequate rest. When you take care of yourself, you are strengthening your ability to cope with challenges.

- Learning from adversity: Instead of seeing challenges as insurmountable obstacles, try to see them as opportunities for growth. Each time you overcome an obstacle, you gain experience and wisdom that make you stronger. Reflect on what you have learned from past difficulties and how you can apply it in the future.

- Seeking support: You are not alone in your journey to resilience. Seek support from other Black women in your community. Sharing your experiences and listening to those of others can be a source of strength. Together, we can overcome anything.

- Visualizing success: Close your eyes and visualize your goals and dreams. Imagine your life full of success and joy. This visualization can help you maintain a positive mindset and keep you focused on what really matters.

I hope these words inspire you to continue developing your resilience. Remember that there is always light at the end of the tunnel, even in the darkest of times. Together, as black women, we are strong and powerful.

Overcoming challenges with grace

Let's talk about grace in the midst of challenges, a topic that touches our lives as black women in profound ways.

Throughout history, we have faced adversity and challenges that have tested our strength and resilience. However, we have also demonstrated exceptional grace in overcoming those obstacles.

Here are some thoughts on how we can approach challenges with grace.

- Holding on to our identity: Our identity as black women is a treasure we carry with grace. Despite adversity, we hold on to our cultural roots and our history with pride. Let us always remember who we are and where we come from, as this gives us the strength to face any challenge.

- Resisting with dignity: Throughout history, we have faced racial and gender discrimination in many forms. However, we have resisted with dignity and determination. Let us always remember that we are worthy of equality and respect, and let us not allow challenges to erode our self-esteem.

- Learning from our foremothers: Many black women who came before we have left a legacy of strength and grace. Their stories and accomplishments are sources of inspiration. By studying and honoring our foremothers, we can learn valuable lessons about meeting challenges with grace and determination.

- Supporting each other: Solidarity among Black women is a powerful source of strength. By supporting each other, we create a network of support that helps us face challenges with grace. Together, we are stronger.

- Cultivating emotional resilience: Emotional resilience is key to overcoming challenges with grace. Let's learn to recognize and manage our emotions in healthy ways. Constructive emotional expression and self-care are tools that can help us stay calm in difficult times.

In our community, we carry an innate grace that has been shaped by our unique experiences.

Let us continue to face challenges with determination, dignity and the grace that characterizes us. Together, we can overcome any obstacle and move forward to a future full of success and joy.

Chapter 4.

Joy and Authenticity

On our journey, we often face challenges and obstacles that can make us feel exhausted, but I want to remind you that joy and authenticity are two treasures we carry within us that can guide us to a fuller and more satisfying life.

Rediscovering joy is like finding a treasure hidden in the deepest corner of our being. In the midst of our struggles and responsibilities, we sometimes forget to allow ourselves to feel joy.

We face a history of pain and oppression, and it may seem that joy is a luxury we cannot afford. However, it is vital to remember that joy is an essential part of our human experience and a powerful tool of resistance.

Joy is not always found in the big moments; it often resides in the little things in life. In a smile shared with a loved one, in the contagious laughter of a child, in a sunset that takes our breath away.

Learning to recognize and celebrate these moments of joy is empowering. It reminds us that we deserve happiness and that we have the ability to find it even in the most difficult circumstances.

Living authentically is a revolutionary act. In a world that sometimes demands that we hide parts of ourselves or follow external rules and expectations, authenticity is an act of courage and resistance.

It's about embracing all parts of ourselves, even those that society may consider "different" or "unusual".

Living authentically empowers us because it allows us to align ourselves with our deepest beliefs and values. It frees us from the need to fit into predefined molds and allows us to create our own narratives.

On this path to authenticity, we may face challenges and judgments, but we will also find deep satisfaction and a sense of fulfillment that comes from being true to ourselves.

It is important to remember that each of us is enough just as we are. We do not need the approval of others to live authentic and joyful lives. Our worth is not determined by external expectations but by the relationship we have with ourselves.

Exercises and questions for reflection

<u>Exercise 1</u>

Celebrating Everyday Joy

Make a list of 3 joyful moments you have had in the past few days, no matter how small or large. Then answer these questions:

1. What made you feel joy in each of those moments?

____

____

2. How did those moments influence your state of mind and well-being?

3. Have you taken the time to recognize and celebrate these moments of joy in the past?

4. How could you incorporate more of these moments of joy into your daily life?

____

____

____

____

____

5. How do you feel as you remember and cherish these moments of joy?

____

____

____

____

____

Exercise 2

Exploring your Authenticity

Take some time to reflect on who you really are and how you present yourself to the world. Then, answer these questions:

1. What aspects of your authenticity do you feel comfortable sharing with others?

____

____

____

____

____

2. Are there parts of yourself that you have hidden or minimized for fear of judgment or criticism?

____

____

____

____

____

3. How do you feel when you show authenticity versus when you hide behind a mask?

____

____

____

____

____

4. Have you experienced situations where showing up authentically has brought you greater satisfaction and connection with others?

____

____

____

____

____

5. What steps could you take to live more authentically in your daily life?

____

____

____

____

____

<u>Exercise 3</u>

Your Journey of Self-Discovery

Create a list of three aspects or personal interests that you feel you have neglected or relegated, either due to external expectations or responsibilities.

Then, answer these questions:

1. Why are these aspects or interests important to you?

____

____

____

____

____

2. How do you feel when you spend time exploring and nurturing these aspects of your identity?

____

____

____

____

____

3. What prevents you from focusing on these aspects?

____

____

____

____

____

4. What actions could you take to prioritize these aspects of yourself?

____

____

____

____

____

5. How do you think your life would be enriched by allowing yourself to fully explore these aspects of your identity?

____

____

____

____

____

Exercise 4

Practicing Gratitude

Each day, take a few minutes to write down 3 things you are grateful for. Then respond:

1. What makes you grateful for these things?

____

____

____

____

____

2. How does practicing gratitude influence your overall outlook and level of joy?

____

____

____

____

____

3. Have you noticed changes in your emotional well-being since you started practicing gratitude?

____

____

____

____

____

4. How does this practice help you maintain a more authentic attitude?

____

____

____

____

____

5. How can you incorporate gratitude into your life more consciously?

____

____

____

____

____

Exercise 5

Writing your Authenticity Manifesto

Take some time to write a brief manifesto that reflects your commitment to living authentically.

Express your values, beliefs and the importance of embracing all parts of yourself.

He then responds:

1. What inspired you to write this manifesto of authenticity?

____

____

____

____

____

2. What are the key values you want to emphasize in your daily life?

____

____

____

____

____

3. How do you plan to remind yourself of the importance of living authentically when facing your challenges?

____

____

____

____

____

4. How do you feel about reading and affirming your authenticity manifesto?

____

____

____

____

____

5. How can you share this manifesto with other black women in your community to inspire a collective sense of authenticity?

____

____

____

____

____

4.1. Rediscovering Joy

In the midst of the struggles and challenges we often face as black women, it is critical for all of us to remember that we have an innate right: joy.

Sometimes, life can lead us down difficult paths, and we may feel our joy fading into the background. But I want you to know that joy is always present, waiting to be rediscovered in our hearts.

Rediscovering joy begins with a deep connection with ourselves. It is an act of self-love that allows us to reconnect with what makes us feel alive and full of energy. It can be as simple as finding joy in small, everyday moments or in the things we are passionate about.

Often, as black women, we carry a burden that we did not choose, but that does not mean we cannot find joy in our lives.

Here are some tips to rediscover joy in your life:

- Connect with your essence: Take time to reflect on who you really are beyond the expectations of others. Find the activities, passions and relationships that make you feel most authentic and alive.

- Practice gratitude: Every day, take a moment to be thankful for the little things. Gratitude can open our hearts to the joy that often goes unnoticed.

- Take care of yourself: Self-care is an act of self-love. Take time to pamper yourself, whether through meditation, exercise, art or any other activity that makes you feel good.

- Surround yourself with love and support: Seek the company of people who understand and support you. Sharing happy moments with friends and family strengthens our emotional connection.

- Embrace the diversity of emotions: Joy doesn't always come without pain or sadness. Learn to embrace all your emotions and allow them to flow. Joy can be even more intense when we experience it after overcoming difficult times.

- Explore and play: Sometimes, joy is hidden in adventure and exploration. Don't be afraid to try new things and follow your passions.

Remember that your joy is a form of resistance and an act of self-love. Don't let anyone take that inner light away from you.

In every smile and laughter, in every achievement and in every day that you embrace with gratitude, you are rediscovering the joy that has always been within you.

4.2. Living authentically

Living authentically as a black woman is a powerful act of resilience and self-love. In a world that often pressures us to be something we are not, finding and embracing our authenticity is a courageous and liberating journey.

Living authentically means being true to yourself in every aspect of your life. It means embracing and celebrating your identity, your experiences and your unique culture.

Here are some reflections on what it means to live authentically as a black woman:

- Embrace your heritage: Your cultural heritage is a valuable part of who you are. Learn about your roots, celebrate your traditions and embrace your identity as a black woman.

- Don't settle: Don't settle for what others expect of you. Define your own values, dreams and goals. You don't have to fit into the molds that others have created.

- Be honest with yourself: Authenticity begins with self-awareness. Reflect on who you really are and what makes you happy. Don't be afraid to face your wants and needs.

- Find your voice: Your voice is powerful. Speak with confidence and stand up for what you believe in. Don't let anyone silence you or make you feel lesser.

- Create meaningful connections: Seek relationships that support and accept you as you are. Authentic friendships and relationships nourish your soul and make you feel valued.

- Celebrate your achievements: Don't minimize your successes or compare yourself to others. Every achievement, big or small, is a manifestation of your authenticity and strength.

- Learn from your challenges: Challenges are part of life, but they are also opportunities to grow and learn. Face obstacles with courage and resilience.

- Inspire others: Your authenticity can inspire other black women to embrace their own authenticity. Share your story and experiences to empower your community.

- Take care of yourself: Self-care is essential to living authentically. Take time to nurture your body, mind and spirit.

- Embrace diversity: Recognize that authenticity manifests itself in many different ways. Accept and celebrate the diversity of black women's experiences around you.

Living authentically as a black woman is a gift you give to yourself and your community.

Remember that you are unique and valuable and that your authenticity is a source of strength and empowerment.

Chapter 5.

Seeking Inner Peace

Amidst the turmoil and chaos of the world around us, seeking inner peace becomes an act of resilience and self-love.

As black women, we often face unique challenges and pressures that can affect our peace of mind and emotional peace.

However, we also possess an incredible capacity to find that peace, nurture it and maintain it, no matter what the circumstances.

Nurturing peace in your life

- Time for yourself: In a world that often expects a lot from us, it is essential to set aside time for self-care. This can include activities that calm you, such as meditation, yoga, dancing or just a quiet moment to read or enjoy your favorite music.

- Connecting with nature: Nature has a powerful calming effect. Take time to be outdoors, even if it's just for a walk in a nearby park. Observe the beauty around you and feel it fill you with serenity.

- Spiritual practices: Spirituality can be a source of peace and strength. Find spiritual practices that resonate with you, whether through religion, meditation, prayer or any other form of connection to the divine.

Maintaining serenity

- Stress Management: Stress is a reality of life for many Black women. Learn effective strategies for managing stress, such as deep breathing, regular exercise and time planning.

- Set boundaries: Learning to say "no" when necessary is critical to maintaining peace. Set clear boundaries in your relationships and commitments to protect your emotional well-being.

- Cultivate gratitude: Practicing gratitude daily can help you maintain a positive outlook and find peace in the midst of difficulties. Take a moment each day to reflect on the things you are grateful for.

- Community support: Seek support from your community, whether through friendships, support groups or shared activities. Mutual support can be a source of strength and peace.

- Forgiveness and release: Learn to forgive and let go of what you cannot control. Forgiveness does not mean accepting mistreatment but freeing yourself from the emotional burden that can affect your inner peace.

Dear sister, inner peace is a gift you deserve. It is a source of strength and empowerment that allows you to face challenges with calm and determination. Cultivating and maintaining that peace is an act of self-love that leads you toward a fuller and more meaningful life.

Exercises and questions for reflection

Here are five exercises related to the theme of seeking inner peace and five questions for each one; read them, exercise them, analyze and answer the questions:

Exercise 1

Your Peace Corner

Find a quiet place in your home or in nature where you can feel at peace. Spend at least 10 minutes a day to be in this place and just breathe and relax. Then, answer these questions:

1. Where is your corner of peace and what makes it special to you?

____

____

____

____

____

2. How do you feel after spending time there?

   ____

   ____

   ____

   ____

   ____

3. What thoughts or worries did you manage to leave behind while you were in your corner of peace?

   ____

   ____

   ____

   ____

   ____

4. How can you incorporate this time of peace into your daily routine?

   ____

   ____

   ____

____

____

5. What other activities can you do in your corner of peace to further nurture your serenity?

____

____

____

____

____

Exercise 2

Gratitude Journal

Each day, write three things you are grateful for in your gratitude journal, big or small, and focus on the positive things in your life.

1. What inspired you to start a gratitude journal?

____

____

____

2. How do you feel as you reflect on the things you are grateful for?

3. Have you noticed any changes in your outlook or mood since you started exercising?

4. What other positive aspects would you like to include?

____

____

____

5. How does this exercise help you maintain inner peace?

____

____

____

____

____

Exercise 3

Conscious Breathing

Spend a few minutes a day practicing conscious breathing.

Sit in a quiet place, close your eyes and concentrate on your breathing.

Inhale deeply for 4 seconds, hold for 4 seconds and then exhale for 4 seconds.

Then, answer these questions:

1. How do you feel before and after practicing conscious breathing?

____

____

____

____

____

2. Do you notice any change in your stress or anxiety level after doing this practice?

____

____

____

____

3. What obstacles do you face in trying to maintain this practice on a regular basis?

____

____

____

---

4. How can you incorporate conscious breathing into your daily life?

5. How do you think mindful breathing can help you maintain serenity?

Exercise 4

Sharing your Inner Peace

Talk to a close friend or loved one about your search for inner peace. Share your experiences, challenges and successes. Then answer these questions:

1. How do you feel about sharing your thoughts and emotions about inner peace with someone close to you?

   ____

   ____

   ____

   ____

   ____

2. What advice or ideas did that person give you to keep you at peace?

   ____

   ____

   ____

____

____

3. Have you learned anything new about yourself through this conversation?

____

____

____

____

____

4. What aspects of the conversation resonated with you and can help you on your journey to inner peace?

____

____

____

____

5. How can you strengthen and maintain connections with people who support you in your quest for peace?

____

____

____

____

____

Exercise 5

Peace Visualization

Close your eyes and visualize a calm and serene place in your mind.

You can be a real or imaginary place. Take a few minutes to fully immerse yourself in this visualization, paying attention to the details and sensations you experience.

Then, answer these questions:

1. What place did you envision and why did you choose it?

   ____

   ____

   ____

   ____

   ____

2. How did you feel during the visualization of this place of peace?

   ____

   ____

   ____

   ____

3. Do you notice any difference in your mood or stress level after the visualization?

   ____

   ____

   ____

____

____

4. How can you use this visualization technique in times of stress or anxiety?

____

____

____

____

____

5. What other places of peace could you explore in future visualizations?

____

____

____

____

____

These exercises and questions are designed to help you seek and maintain inner peace in your daily life.

Reflecting on your experience will help you strengthen your connection to serenity and emotional well-being.

5.1. Nurturing peace in your life

Nurturing peace in your life is an act of self-love and empowerment that we all deserve. In our journey, we often face challenges and moments of turmoil, but we also have the ability to cultivate an inner space of serenity and tranquility.

Let me share some words of support and guidance on how to nurture that peace in your life:

- Find time for yourself: We know how busy our lives can be, but it is essential to set aside regular time to be with yourself. Whether it's meditating, reading, taking a relaxing bath or simply breathing deeply, this time is an investment in your emotional well-being.
- Connect with nature: Mother Nature gives us a constant gift of beauty and peace. Go for a walk in the park, sit under a tree or enjoy the sunset.

Connecting with nature can recharge your spirit and bring you a deep sense of peace.

- Practice self-care: Self-care is not selfish; it is a necessity. Be sure to take care of your body, mind and spirit on a consistent basis. This can include healthy eating, regular exercise and activities that make you happy.

- Set healthy boundaries: Learning to say "no" when necessary is an act of self-love. Set clear boundaries with people and situations that may affect your peace of mind and don't hesitate to protect your peace of mind.

- Cultivate gratitude: Despite the challenges we face, there is always something to be grateful for. Keep a gratitude journal where you can record the positive things in your life. Gratitude can nourish your heart and remind you of the blessings you have.

- Seek support: Sometimes, maintaining inner peace means seeking help from others. Don't hesitate to seek support from friends, family or mental health professionals if needed. Sharing your thoughts and feelings can be liberating.

- Practice authenticity: Living authentically is a source of peace in itself. Don't be afraid to be who you really are and embrace your values and beliefs. Authenticity will lead to greater inner peace.

- Forgive yourself: We all make mistakes and face difficult times. Instead of blaming yourself, practice self-compassion. Learn to forgive yourself and embrace yourself as you are, don't judge yourself, accept yourself, forgive yourself, love yourself and value yourself.

- Find moments of silence: Silence can be healing. Take time to be quiet, either through meditation or just sitting in peace. Silence can help you find answers and recharge.

- Practice patience: Inner peace is not achieved overnight. It is an ongoing journey. Be patient with yourself as you work on nurturing your inner peace. Each small step brings you closer to a more serene and fulfilling life.

Remember that you deserve to live a life filled with peace and well-being. No matter how hectic the world around you is, your inner peace is a refuge to which you can always return.

Keep that spark of serenity alive in your heart and allow it to guide you in your quest for empowerment and fulfillment.

5.2. Maintaining serenity

Maintaining serenity in the midst of life's storms can sometimes seem like an overwhelming challenge, but I want to remind you that within you resides an incredible force that can bring you peace and balance in any situation.

Let me share some words of support and guidance on how to maintain serenity in your life:

- Know yourself: The key to maintaining serenity is self-knowledge. Take the time to explore your thoughts, emotions and personal triggers. The better you know yourself, the easier it will be to stay calm.

- Practice conscious breathing: Breathing is a powerful tool for finding serenity. When you feel overwhelmed, take a few moments to breathe deeply. Inhale calmness and exhale tension.

- Cultivate acceptance: Accepting the things you cannot change is fundamental to serenity. Life sometimes presents us with challenges, but learning to accept what you cannot control will free you from distress.

- Set clear boundaries: Don't hesitate to set healthy boundaries with people and situations that may disturb your peace. Learn to say "no" when necessary and protect your serenity with determination.

- Find time for self-care: Self-care is essential to maintaining serenity. Make time for activities that bring you joy and peace, whether it's meditating, reading a good book or taking a relaxing walk.

- Practice gratitude: Focusing on the blessings you have in your life can bring serenity. Keep a gratitude journal where you can remember the positive things around you.

- Seek support: Talking to friends, family members or mental health professionals can be a source of support and comfort. Don't face difficulties alone; seek help when you need it.

- Find moments of silence: In the midst of noise and chaos, seek moments of silence. Whether through meditation or simply sitting in peace, silence can nurture your inner serenity.

- Practice patience: Serenity is not achieved overnight. It is an ongoing journey. Be patient with yourself as you work on maintaining serenity in your life.

- Remember your inner strength: Never underestimate the strength that lies within you. You have the ability to overcome challenges and maintain composure in the midst of adversity.

Your serenity is a precious gift that you deserve to keep. No matter how turbulent the world around you is, you can find a haven of calm within you.

Trust in your strength and continue to seek serenity in your life; you deserve to live with peace and balance.

Chapter 6.

Sustainable Self-Care

A topic we often overlook but which is of utmost importance to our well-being is sustainable self-care.

In a world where we are constantly faced with challenges and responsibilities, we sometimes forget to take care of ourselves in a way that lasts and nourishes our souls.

Let me share some thoughts on how we can prioritize our wellness and create a life of continuous self-care.

Prioritizing your well-being

- Learn to say "yes" to yourself: Too often, we say "yes" to external demands and "no" to our own needs. Prioritizing your well-being involves learning to say "yes" to yourself and recognizing that you deserve time and attention.

- Set healthy boundaries: Boundaries are essential for sustainable self-care. Don't be afraid to say "no" when necessary and protect your emotional energy. Your boundaries are an act of self-love.

- Cultivate self-awareness: Knowing yourself is essential to knowing what you need. Take the time to explore your emotions, thoughts and desires. Self-awareness will help you identify your needs and how to meet them.

- Incorporate self-care into your routine: Instead of viewing self-care as an additional chore, integrate it into your daily routine. Small acts of self-care, such as taking a few minutes to meditate or enjoying a cup of tea, can make a big difference.

Towards a life of continuous self-care

- Create a personalized self-care plan: Design a self-care plan that is unique to you. Identify the activities and practices that nourish you and make you feel good. Your self-care plan should be a guide that you can follow throughout your life.

- Commitment to yourself: Sustainable self-care involves an ongoing commitment to yourself. It's not something you do occasionally but a lifestyle you embrace constantly.
- Find support: Seek out a supportive community of black women who value and encourage self-care. Boards can inspire each other and share strategies for staying sustainable.
- Adapt your self-care: Life is full of changes, and your self-care plan should be flexible. As you face different stages and challenges, adjust your self-care so that it remains relevant and effective.
- Remember your worth: Ultimately, sustainable self-care is a constant reminder of your worth. You deserve to consistently and lovingly take care of yourself, no matter the circumstances.

Sustainable self-care is an act of self-love that we must embrace. It is not selfishness; it is a necessity. By prioritizing our wellness and creating a life of continuous self-care, we strengthen our ability to face challenges with grace and empowerment.

I encourage you to make self-care an integral part of your life and always remember that you deserve to give yourself all the love and care possible; I recommend you make this, from this moment on, an unwavering lifelong commitment.

Exercises and questions for reflection

<u>Exercise 1</u>

Design your personalized self-care plan

Take some time to reflect on the activities and self-care practices that nourish you and make you feel good.

Then, create a personalized self-care plan that is tailored to your needs.

This plan should be a guide that you can follow throughout your life.

1. What are the self-care activities that make you feel better about yourself?

____

____

____

____

____

2. How do you feel after practicing these activities?

____

____

____

____

____

3. How often do you consider it appropriate to incorporate these practices into your routine?

____

____

____

____

____

4. How do you plan to integrate your plan into your daily life?

____

____

____

____

____

5. How will you remind yourself to follow your self-care plan?

____

____

____

____

____

Exercise 2

Commitment to yourself

Reflect on the importance of ongoing commitment to self-care. What does it mean to you to commit to sustainable self-care? Write down your reflections and commitments.

1. What does commitment to yourself mean in the context of sustainable self-care?

____

____

____

____

____

2. What are the specific areas in which you want to become more engaged?

____

____

____

____

____

3. How do you feel about committing to self-care?

____

____

____

____

____

4. What are the barriers that could hinder your engagement, and how do you plan to overcome them?

____

____

____

____

____

5. What concrete steps will you take to maintain an ongoing commitment to yourself in your self-care journey?

____

____

____

____

____

<u>Exercise 3</u>

Find your support community.

Research and find a community of black women who share your values of sustainable self-care.

It can be online or in person.

Join this community...

Actively participates in discussions and activities related to self-care.

1. How did you discover this support community?

____

____

____

____

____

2. What self-care resources and discussions did you find most helpful in this community?

____

____

____

____

____

3. How do you feel about connecting with other black women who value self-care?

____

____

____

____

____

4. What lessons or advice have you learned from other women in the community?

____

____

____

____

____

5. How do you plan to maintain your active participation in this community over time?

____

____

____

____

____

Exercise 4

Adapt your self-care

Think about a time when you faced a significant change in your life, such as a new job, a relationship or a move. Reflect on how you adapted your self-care in that situation.

1. What significant change did you face in your life?

____

____

____

____

2. How did that change affect your self-care routine?

____

____

____

____

____

3. What specific adjustments did you make in your self-care to adapt to the situation?

____

____

____

____

____

4. What did you learn about self-care adaptation during that period of change?

____

____

____

____

____

5. How will you apply those lessons in future change situations?

____

____

____

____

____

Exercise 5

Remember your worth

Write a letter to yourself constantly reminding yourself of your worth and the importance of self-care in your life.

Be kind to yourself and recognize that you deserve unwavering love and care.

1. What message would you like to remind yourself of your worth?

____

____

____

____

____

2. How do you feel about writing this letter of self-love?

____

____

____

____

____

3. What words of encouragement would you give yourself in moments of self-reflection?

____

____

____

____

____

4. What is the role of self-care in constantly reminding you of your worth?

____

____

____

____

____

5. Where will you place this card to remind yourself of its importance?

____

____

____

____

____

I hope these exercises and questions inspire you to embrace sustainable self-care as an ongoing, loving commitment to yourself.

Remember that self-care is a manifestation of self-love and a powerful tool to keep us strong and resilient on our journey to empowerment and wholeness.

6.1. Prioritizing your well-being

Prioritizing your well-being is an act of self-love and resilience in a world that often tries to rob us of our peace and happiness.

As black women, we face unique challenges, and it is essential that we take care of ourselves on a consistent and sustainable basis.

Now, I want to talk to you about the importance of prioritizing your emotional, mental and physical well-being. Sometimes, we can feel overwhelmed by external expectations and responsibilities, but remember that taking care of yourself is not a luxury, it's a necessity.

Here are some strategies and tips to make sure you're at the top of your priority list.

I will discuss how to set healthy boundaries, learn to say "no" when necessary, and how to embrace self-care as an act of empowerment.

Remember that taking care of yourself is a revolutionary act. In doing so, you strengthen yourself and become a beacon of light and resistance for your community and yourself.

Let's continue together on this journey of sustainable self-care, where every step you take is a testament to your self-love and your determination to live a life full of joy and authenticity.

Here are some ideas, strategies and tips to make sure you are at the top of your priority list:

- Set healthy boundaries: Setting boundaries is a powerful way to take care of yourself. Learn to say "no" when you feel a request or commitment is not aligned with your needs or values. Acknowledge your boundaries and communicate them clearly but kindly. Don't feel guilty about protecting your time and energy.

- Practice the Art of Selective "Yes": Saying "yes" to everything can lead to burnout and overload. Learn to carefully select which projects or activities you want to get involved in. Consider whether an opportunity brings you joy, personal growth or genuine benefits before committing.

- Embrace Self-Care: Self-care is an act of love for yourself. Make time regularly to take care of your physical and emotional well-being. This can include activities such as meditating, exercising, enjoying a relaxing bath or simply resting. Find what nourishes you and make it a priority in your life.

- Learning to delegate: Often, we believe we should do everything ourselves. However, learning to delegate tasks and responsibilities can free up time and reduce the burden. Whether at work, at home or in your community, consider who else could handle certain tasks.

- Seek Support and Community: You are not alone in this journey. Seek support from other Black women who share your experiences and challenges. This can be a network of close female friends, support groups or online communities. Sharing your experiences and learning from others can be a powerful source of strength.

- Practice Self-Compassion: Treat yourself with the same kindness and compassion you would show a loved one. Allow yourself to make mistakes and learn from them. Self-compassion helps you stay balanced and get through difficult times with grace.

- Evaluate and Adjust Regularly: Life is constantly changing, and what works one moment may need adjustment later. Take the time to periodically evaluate your priorities and needs. Adjust your focus as needed to maintain a healthy balance.

Remember that taking care of yourself is an act of empowerment. In doing so, you strengthen yourself to face challenges and live a fulfilling life.

You are worthy of love and care, and you deserve to be at the top of your own priority list.

6.2. Towards a life of continuous self-care

On our path to emotional self-care, empowerment and wholeness, one of the most valuable lessons we can learn is the importance of our ongoing self-care.

As black women, we often find ourselves playing multiple roles and facing challenges, and this can lead us to neglect ourselves. But you must remember that you deserve to take care of yourself on an ongoing basis, not just in times of crisis.

Self-care is not a selfish act but an act of self-love and resilience. It means taking deliberate and conscious steps to maintain your emotional, mental and physical well-being over time. It is not just a one-time event but an ongoing commitment to yourself.

Here, you will find strategies and tips for integrating self-care into your daily life. You will learn how to identify signs of burnout, establish self-care routines that will work for you, and surround yourself with a supportive community to encourage you on this journey.

To that end, let's talk about how you can integrate self-care into your daily life in a way that is meaningful and sustainable. As black women, we often face unique challenges and therefore, it is critical to learn how to consistently take care of ourselves.

These are some of the strategies and practical tips that will help you have a fuller and more balanced life:

- Identifying the Signs of Burnout: One of the first steps on the path to self-care is to be aware of the signs of burnout. Pay attention to your body and mind. Do you constantly feel tired? Do you find it hard to concentrate or sleep? Do you experience physical symptoms, such as headaches or muscle tension? These are signs that you may be neglecting your emotional and physical well-being.

- Establishing Self-Care Routines: Self-care is not just about indulgent and sporadic treatments but about incorporating regular practices into your life. Start by identifying what activities bring you joy and relaxation, such as meditating, walking outdoors, enjoying a relaxing bath or practicing yoga. Establish a daily or weekly routine for these activities and respect them as appointments with yourself.
- Creating a Community of Support: Sharing your self-care journey with other black women can be a valuable source of support and motivation. Seek out support groups, online communities or friends who share your wellness goals. Sharing your experiences and challenges will remind you that you are not alone; there are others just like us, and this will provide you with valuable advice.
- Setting Clear Boundaries: Sometimes self-care involves saying "no" in a firm but kind way. Learn

to set clear boundaries with others and advocate for your time and energy. This will allow you to prioritize your needs without feeling guilty.

- Planning Self-Care Strategically: Strategic planning is key to integrating self-care into your busy life. Create a self-care plan that includes your priority practices, as well as times for rest and relaxation. Organize your schedule according to your wellness priorities.

- Learning from Experiences: Remember that self-care is an evolving process. As you progress, you will learn what works best for you and what does not. Don't be afraid to adjust your routines and explore new self-care practices as you grow and change.

Your emotional and physical well-being is a priority. Integrating self-care into your daily life is an act of self-love and empowerment. Not only will you benefit, but you will also be a role model for future generations of black women who will learn the importance of taking care of themselves.

Remember that taking care of yourself is an act of resilience. It is a constant reminder of your worth and strength. By doing so, you not only benefit yourself but also inspire other black women to do the same.

I encourage you to make this a constant commitment and celebrate every small victory on your journey to a life of fulfillment and well-being.

Conclusion of Volume II

As we come to the end of Volume II and the book, our journey to emotional wellness and empowerment has been a journey full of learning, self-discovery and growth.

Together we explore strategies for maintaining inner calm, releasing emotions constructively, developing resilience, rediscovering joy and living authentically.

Throughout these chapters, we have reflected on the importance of continuous self-care and how to nurture our inner peace in the midst of adversity.

I shared exercises, tips and experiences that I hope have enriched your life and helped you to strengthen your emotional well-being.

It is critical to remember that the path to empowerment and fulfillment is continuous. Every day is a new opportunity to grow, heal and thrive. This is why I encourage you to take with you the lessons learned on this journey and apply them in your daily life.

Our commitment to self-care and the pursuit of inner peace is an act of self-love and an act of resilience. As black women, we face unique challenges, but we also have unwavering strength and resilience.

I invite you to continue to build a community of support, share your stories and inspire other black women to join this journey of empowerment and self-care. Together, we are stronger.

Thus concludes Volume II of our journey to emotional self-care. But remember that this is not the end but the beginning of a life in which your inner peace, joy and authenticity are priorities.

I thank you for allowing me to be part of your journey and I hope we continue to grow together.

Bonus

Bonus 1. Self-care exercises

As part of our ongoing commitment to emotional wellness and empowerment, I prepared this Bonus 1: Self-Care Exercises so you can continue to strengthen your relationship with yourself.

These exercises are simple yet powerful and are designed to nourish your mind, body and spirit.

<u>Exercise 1</u>

The Love Letter to Yourself

Write a love letter to yourself. Express all the love, gratitude and appreciation you feel for the amazing person you are.

Read the letter aloud in front of the mirror and allow yourself to feel the flow of self-love.

Exercise 2

Digital Disconnect Day

Dedicate a full day to disconnect from electronic devices. Use this time to reconnect with nature, enjoy activities you are passionate about or simply relax without digital distractions.

Exercise 3

Healing Bath Ritual

Prepare a special bath with bath salts, essential oils and scented candles.

Immerse yourself in the bathtub and let the water envelop you.

As you bathe, visualize that all your tensions and worries are dissolving in the water.

<u>Exercise 4</u>

Gratitude Meditation

Create a quiet space in your home and sit in a comfortable position.

Close your eyes and practice a gratitude meditation session.

Think of three things you are grateful for today.

Let gratitude fully fill your whole heart.

<u>Exercise 5</u>

Dance and Body Expression

Play your favorite music and dance without restrictions.

Allow yourself to feel the music in your body and express your emotions through movement. Dance is a powerful way to release energy and experience joy.

Each of these exercises is designed to take care of yourself and maintain your emotional well-being.

Don't forget that self-care is an act of self-love, and you deserve these moments of healing and rejuvenation.

I hope you enjoy these self-care exercises and continue your journey towards emotional self-care, empowerment and wholeness with love and compassion.

Bonus 2. Finding and creating a supportive community

On our path to empowerment and emotional well-being, the support of a community is invaluable.

Here's Bonus 2: Finding and Creating a Community of Support. Connecting with other Black women who share our experiences and challenges can enrich our lives in deep and meaningful ways.

<u>Exercise 1</u>

Identifying Existing Communities

Research and list black women's communities online or in your local area.

This could include seeking out social networking groups, non-profit organizations, book clubs, support groups, among others.

Then, review your list carefully and answer the following questions.

This will help you make a decision as to what is the best option for you at this time.

1. Which communities catch your attention?

2. What types of black women's communities exist in your area or online?

3. What topics would you like to explore in the community?

4. Do you have friends or acquaintances who might be involved in these communities?

5. What is your main motivation for joining and belonging to a black women's community?

<u>Exercise 2</u>

Active Participation

Once you have identified a community that interests you, participate actively.

Join events, online discussions or local activities.

Establish genuine connections and share your experiences and knowledge.

1. How do you feel about belonging and participating in this community?

   ____

   ____

   ____

   ____

   ____

2. Have you found new friendships or made meaningful connections within this new community?

   ____

   ____

____

____

____

3. How do they contribute to the community and how do they benefit them?

____

____

____

____

____

4. What challenges, if any, have you experienced being part of this community?

____

____

____

____

____

<u>Exercise 3</u>

Create your own community.

If you don't find a community that fits your needs, consider creating your own.

Invite black women you know or who share your interests to join.

Organize events, activities or meetings that foster mutual support and connection.

Then answer the questions I show you below:

1. What kind of community would you like to create?

____

____

____

____

____

2. How can you attract other black women to join?

____

____

____

____

____

3. What are the key objectives and values of your community?

____

____

____

____

____

4. How do you envision this community benefiting its members?

____

____

____

____

____

<u>Exercise 4</u>

The Power of Collaboration

Explore ways to collaborate with other communities or like-minded groups. Collaboration can enrich your experiences and broaden your perspectives.

1. What collaboration opportunities do you see available?

____

____

____

____

____

2. What could you bring to a collaboration?

____

____

____

____

____

3. How would your community and other communities benefit from this collaboration?

____

____

____

____

____

4. What are your short- and long-term goals for this collaboration?

____

____

____

____

____

<u>Exercise 5</u>

Ongoing Support

Maintain and nurture your connections in the support community of your choice.

You can do this either as one of the active members of the community you have joined or as the leader of the community you have formed.

Mutual support is a constant source of strength and empowerment.

1. How do you plan to maintain and strengthen your connections in the community?

   ____

   ____

   ____

   ____

   ____

2. What positive changes have you experienced in your life as a result of the community?

   ____

   ____

   ____

   ____

3. What are your long-term goals for your community involvement?

____

____

____

____

____

The power of community is transformative, and by coming together as black women, we can create a space where empowerment and emotional well-being flourish.

Don't underestimate the impact you can have on the lives of others and yourself by finding or creating a community of support.

Together, we are stronger!

Bonus 3. Your Personalized Self-Care Plan: Guide to creating your own plan, templates and examples

In our journey towards self-care, emotional well-being and empowerment, it is crucial to have a personalized self-care plan.

Bonus 3: Your Personalized Self-Care Plan will guide you through the process of creating a plan that is tailored to your unique needs as a black woman.

Here I give you a step-by-step guide, templates and examples to get you started.

Step 1: Personal Reflection

Before creating your plan, take some time to reflect on your emotional needs and what brings you peace and joy, then answer these questions:

1. What activities or practices make you feel more calm and happy?

____

____

____

____

____

2. What are your most frequent emotional challenges?

____

____

____

____

____

3. What kind of support or resources do you need to maintain your emotional well-being?

____

____

____

____

____

4. What is your main goal in creating a self-care plan?

____

____

____

____

____

<u>Step 2</u>: Identify your self-care activities

Make a list of specific activities that will help you relax, recharge your energy and strengthen your emotional well-being.

These activities can range from meditating to exercising, enjoying nature, reading, journaling or simply resting.

Use this template for your list of self-care activities:

Self-care activity 1: _____________________

Self-care activity 2: _____________________

Self-care activity 3: ____________________

Self-care activity 4: ____________________

Self-care activity 5: ____________________

<u>Step 3</u>: Prioritize your activities

Rank self-care activities according to their importance to you.

- Which ones are essential to your emotional well-being?
- Which ones are optional but still valuable?

This classification will help you establish a clear focus.

Use this template to prioritize your self-care activities:

Esencial:

____

Important:

____

Worthy:

____

<u>Step 4</u>: Create a Self-Care Calendar

Make regular time for self-care activities.

They can be daily, weekly or monthly.

Be sure to schedule these activities in your calendar as appointments with yourself.

Use this template for your self-care calendar:

- Monday:

____

- Tuesday:

____

- Wednesday:

____

- Thursday:

____

- Friday:

____

- Saturday:

____

- Sunday:

____

<u>Step 5</u>: Adjust and Revise Your Plan

As you go through your self-care journey, it is normal for your needs to change.

Review and adjust your plan as needed.

Add new activities, eliminate those that no longer benefit you and be flexible with yourself.

Creating your own personalized self-care plan is an act of love for yourself. Remember that you deserve to take care of yourself and prioritize your emotional well-being.

With this plan, you will be better equipped to face the challenges and celebrate the joys of life.

Below are several examples of self-care plans, which you can use as guides to develop your own plan:

Example 1 for Personalized Self-Care Plan

<u>Step 1</u>: Personal Reflection

Emotional needs: I often feel stressed because of my job and family responsibilities. I also experienced times of emotional exhaustion.

What brings me peace and joy: I enjoy meditation, reading and spending time outdoors. Being with close friends and my family makes me feel loved and supported.

Recurring emotional challenges: Dealing with work stress, finding time for myself and balancing my family responsibilities.

<u>Step 2</u>: Self-Care Activities

- Daily meditation for 15 minutes.
- Read at least one chapter of a book I like every night before going to sleep.
- Nature walks on weekends.
- Have a family game night every Friday.

- Date with a close friend once a month to chat and relax.

Step 3: Prioritization

- Essential self-care activity: Daily meditation.
- Important self-care activities: Reading before bedtime and spending time in nature.
- Valuable self-care activities: Family game night and dates with friends.

Step 4: Self-Care Calendar

- Monday: Meditation.
- Tuesday: Meditation.
- Wednesday: Meditation.
- Thursday: Meditation.
- Friday: Meditation and family game night.
- Saturday: Nature walk.
- Sunday: Bedtime reading.

Step 5: Adjustments and Revisions

After a month, I noticed that meditation helped me reduce stress. I decided to increase the duration of meditation to 20 minutes.

I changed the family game night to Saturday due to the availability of all family members.

This is just one example: your Personalized Self-Care Plan should be tailored to your specific needs and preferences.

Remember that you can adjust it at any time as your circumstances and emotional needs change.

Here is another example:

Example 2 for Personalized Self-Care Plan

<u>Step 1</u>: Personal Reflection

Emotional needs: I often feel overwhelmed by anxiety due to work and family demands.

I also experienced episodes of sadness and exhaustion.

What brings me peace and joy: Practicing yoga, creating art and having moments of creative solitude.

Recurring emotional challenges: Dealing with anxiety, finding time for myself, and balancing my roles as a mother and professional.

Step 2: Self-Care Activities

- Yoga at home for 30 minutes 3 times a week.
- Reserve one afternoon a month for an art workshop.
- Practice mindfulness meditation for 10 minutes every morning.
- Set boundaries at work and say "no" when necessary.
- Spend an hour alone in a quiet space once a week.

Step 3: Prioritization

- Essential self-care activity: Yoga at home.
- Important self-care activities: Monthly art workshop and daily meditation.
- Valuable self-care activities: Establish boundaries at work and alone time.

<u>Step 4</u>: Self-Care Calendar

- Monday: Yoga at home.
- Tuesday: Mindfulness meditation.
- Wednesday: Yoga at home.
- Thursday: Mindfulness meditation.
- Friday: Yoga at home.
- Saturday: Art workshop.
- Sunday: Time alone.

<u>Step 5</u>: Adjustments and Revisions

After a month, I noticed that yoga at home helped me reduce my anxiety.

I decided to add an additional session on Sunday afternoons.

By setting boundaries at work, I can better manage my workload and reduce the feeling of burnout.

Remember that this plan is customized and can be modified according to your needs and change over time.

The important thing is that it provides you with the self-care necessary to maintain your emotional well-being.

Link to the Black Women's Wellness Foundation platform.

https://www.ffbww.org/

On this platform you will find support, community and support for you and your specific circumstances.

Your help means a lot

If you liked this book, one of the best things you could do for me would be to leave a review on the website where you bought it. It won't take you long, but it would be great if you could spare those minutes for me.

If you give my work a high rating, more people will see it and, in turn, it will improve their lives, health and happiness.

May your journey be filled with peace, health and abundance,

Malaika Ndiaye

www.ingramcontent.com/pod-product-compliance
Lightning Source LLC
Chambersburg PA
CBHW050744150726
48196CB00003B/346